MEXICO'S
ROSWELL

The Chihuahua UFO Crash

By
Noe Torres and Ruben Uriarte

With an Afterword By Stanton T. Friedman,
Nuclear Physicist and Original Roswell Investigator

"Mexico's Roswell," by Noe Torres and Ruben Uriarte. ISBN 978-1-60264-013-9.

Library of Congress Control Number: 2007926364.

Manufactured in the United States of America.

TABLE OF CONTENTS

DEDICATION:

Noe Torres: In memory of my mother, Maria de Jesus Torres, whose chilling story of a UFO encounter on a dark night in a South Texas orange grove remains with me to this day.

Ruben Uriarte: To my family, loved ones, friends and fellow researchers who have guided me on my journey

PROLOGUE

"All that we see or seem, is but a dream within a dream."
                                                    -Edgar Allan Poe.

Emitting an enormous, billowing cloud of dust behind it, the 1993 GMC Suburban shook and groaned as it bounced along a rugged, desolate dirt road in the Chihuahuan Desert about 50 miles north of Coyame, Mexico. Within the wildly vibrating interior of the sport utility vehicle, we, the authors of this book, and our entourage struggled in vain to maintain a firm grip on our digital cameras, GPS receivers, handheld computers, and other possessions. The day had been a difficult one for us, with many hours spent exploring this vast stretch of sun-drenched desert. Now finally, we were approaching the very place where our research indicated that a small airplane collided with an unidentified flying object, causing both aircraft to spiral out of control onto the desert below, on August 25, 1974.

As we turned a corner, our guide Martin Sanchez suddenly put the brakes on, and the SUV skidded to a stop on the hard, rocky dirt road. Señor Pedro Venegas, who had joined our quest after we stopped to ask directions at his ranch nearby, pointed eagerly through the front windshield at a large gap that was visible between two nearby mountains ahead of us. *"Allí está!* There it is!" He exclaimed, "Right between these mountains, you can see *El Llano*."

Shimmering in the desert sun ahead of us lay a vast white plain that extends for over 100 miles, north to south, and just beyond the plain, we could see the hazy magnificence of the *Sierra La Esperanza* mountain range, immediately to the east of which is the Rio Grande River and the international boundary separating Mexico from the United States of America. Reacting to the spectacular view of *El Llano*, I found myself saying, "Oh, my God. I had no idea it was so immense." Spread across the desert floor before us like a translucent white carpet, this expanse of flatness between mountains was the stage where one of the dramatic moments in human history is said to have occurred on a warm summer night in 1974.

1

As we sat inside our vehicle for a few moments, taking in the breathtaking panorama around us, the feeling grew deep inside me that we had arrived at a place of special importance. "My God, this is the place," I told the others. "We are right here where the U.S. helicopters from El Paso flew in to recover the crashed UFO."

Our First View of "El Llano" (2007 by Ruben Uriarte)

Suddenly we all scrambled outside of the SUV to take photographs and gather in more of the feeling and flavor of this extraordinary place. I turned to Señor Venegas and asked, "Just over that mountain range is the Rio Grande River?"

"*Sí*," he replied, "There is actually a road that you can take with a four-wheel drive that goes over that mountain and right up to the river. From there, you cross on a raft, and you're in Ruiodosa, Texas. A little bit north of there is Candelaria, Texas."

As we scanned the vastness of the nearby plain, he turned to me and said, "If those helicopters wanted to get out of Mexico fast without any trouble, this would be the perfect place." Pointing to *Sierra La Esperanza*, he added, "Right over those mountains."

Standing in the early afternoon sun in Mexico's Chihuahuan Desert on this clear, cool day in January 2007, the members of our UFO investigation team quietly struggled to grasp the full significance of what occurred near the very place where we stood. The crash of a flying disk and a small airplane near this very spot is

2

often referred to as the most significant UFO event since the Roswell saucer crash of 1947. Gilberto E. Rivera, one of Mexico's leading UFO researchers, calls the Coyame incident "comparable in scope to the July 1947 UFO crash near Roswell."

Dubbed "Mexico's Roswell," the mid-air collision near Coyame of an airplane and a UFO has been the subject of a major documentary by *The History Channel* in 2005 and numerous articles in newspapers, magazines, and Web sites. As more information comes to light about it, UFO researchers say, the Coyame case might one day be viewed as being of even more significance than Roswell.

Airplane Fragments We Found Near Coyame (2007 by Ruben Uriarte)

During our investigative visit to *El Llano*, we uncovered many strange things. We heard countless eerie stories told by the humble people who inhabit the region's small towns and villages. Coyame resident Leandro Valeriano told me, "We know that strange things sometimes come out of the sky, and they can harm you. They are dangerous to approach."

In this book, we will look closely at the events of the last week of August 1974, when this rugged, lonely stretch of desert near the Mexico-Texas border suddenly became a whirlwind of activity, as two governments raced to recover the remnants of what was perhaps a vehicle sent to our planet by entities not of this Earth. In this most unlikely of places for such high drama to unfold, some believe that the UFO-airplane collision may have unleashed a form of alien bacteriological or chemical contamination that may have cost the lives of as many as 24 Mexican soldiers.

The story of what happened in 1974 near the tiny Mexican town of Coyame, Chihuahua, rivals the most intensely exciting science-fiction tale ever created, and yet those of us who have studied it carefully have the distinct suspicion that it is *not* fiction. Although concrete physical proof is, for the time being, lacking, this amazing story continues to captivate the imaginations of thousands of people on both sides of the U.S. border with Mexico.

Was this crashed UFO a visitor from the stars? Skeptics argue that extraterrestrial travel cannot happen, and the authors fully conceded it is not possible ... *for the human race in our present time*. But, what if we are being visited by members of civilizations that are, say, 1,000 years more advanced than we are? What was our own earth like 1,000 years ago? Europe was steeped in the Middle Ages, the Viking Age was at its height, and the Chinese were beginning experimentation with gunpowder. A time traveler carrying cell phones, handheld computers, digital cameras, and other commonplace modern devices would certainly be immediately burned at the stake. Furthermore, what if the UFO occupants are from a civilization 5,000 years more advanced than us – or perhaps even 10,000 years? It is the height of human egotism to believe that our race is currently the most highly advanced species in the cosmos.

Interestingly, less than three months after the reported crash of the UFO near Coyame, Mexico, the human race made its first deliberate, scientific effort to beam a message from earth to whomever might be eavesdropping elsewhere in the galaxy. On the afternoon of November 16, 1974, the world's largest radio telescope, located at the Arecibo Observatory in Puerto Rico, broadcast humanity's first message specifically directed at other intelligent life in the universe. And what did we have to say when we first grabbed the microphone and delivered an appeal to be allowed into the exclusive club of the highly advanced civilizations of the cosmos? The simple message contained representations of the fundamental chemicals of life, the formula for DNA, a crude diagram of our solar system, and outline pictures of a human being and the Arecibo telescope.

In another striking coincidence, almost exactly three years to the day of the reported Coyame UFO crash, an astronomer at Ohio State University's *Big Ear* radio telescope intercepted a mysterious signal from outer space that scientists to this day consider to be the most likely candidate to have originated from an extraterrestrial intelligence. After detecting the strong narrowband radio signal from outer space on August 15, 1977, Dr. Jerry R. Ehman marked the computer printout of the event with the single word, "Wow!" It has been known as the *Wow! Signal* ever since. Why has a similar signal not been detected since then? Some have speculated that the strange signal may not have come from as far away as astronomers thought and that we may have accidentally tapped into a two-way conversation between UFOs traveling within our own solar system.

Skeptics also argue that if UFOs really exist, somebody somewhere would have obtained a tangible piece of real evidence, such as a fragment of a flying disk. Then again, how careful would *we* be if we were visiting and studying a culture that was 10,000 years less advanced than we are? For us to somehow make our presence widely known to them (1) would ruin our mission of observing them in their own element, and (2) would likely lead to extreme instability and possible catastrophe for the contaminated species.

UFO researchers routinely accuse government authorities of suppressing information that would prove these objects really do exist. Persons who believe this way are viewed as part of a lunatic fringe. However, beyond the hard-core conspiracy theorists that see a government cover-up behind every paranormal event, there is a large number of tangible, credible individuals from all walks of life who strongly believe that historically it serves the authorities in power best not to disclose the existence of data or artifacts that would prove the existence of intelligent civilizations not of the earth.

Such worldview-shattering knowledge, regardless of whether it results in an overall positive or negative effect on society in the long run, would certainly create short-term turmoil and instability in our society's long held norms, beliefs, and institutions. If the conviction of thousands in the 1960s that women and minorities should be treated more fairly caused such social upheaval, can you imagine the changes that might ensue after a sudden announcement that we are not alone in the universe and that extraterrestrials have been observing and studying our race for many, many years?

As Edgar Allan Poe wondered, "Is all that we see or seem but a dream within a dream?" We challenge our readers to read this book with the same sense of wonder. Let us concede the possibility, however frightening, that there may be unseen forces at work in the universe around us that we do not yet fully understand. "The beginning of wisdom is the discovery of one's own ignorance," Socrates said. If UFOs are not extraterrestrial spacecraft, perhaps they are something else. Scoff at your own risk and continue to call them folktales of the ignorant, if doing so helps you return unchanged to your everyday existence.

If you are inclined to believe or to at least keep an open mind, you are not alone. The great and powerful men of the world have wondered right along with you what these strange luminous disks in the night skies are. Before becoming the U.S. President, Jimmy Carter said, "I don't laugh at people anymore when they say they've seen UFOs. I've seen one myself. It was the darnedest thing I have ever seen. It was big, it was bright, it changed colors and it was about the size of the moon." Later, while campaigning for President, he told the news media, "I am convinced that UFOs exist because I have seen one."

Another U.S. President, Harry S. Truman, stated in 1950, "I can assure you that flying saucers, given that they exist, are not constructed by any power on earth."

Roscoe H. Hillenkoetter, director of the Central Intelligence Agency from 1947 to 1950, told the *New York Times*, "Behind the scenes, high-ranking Air Force officers are soberly concerned about the UFOs. But through official secrecy and ridicule, many citizens are led to believe the unknown flying objects are nonsense. To hide the facts, the Air Force has silenced its personnel."

6

NASA astronaut L. Gordon Cooper stated, "I believe that these extraterrestrial vehicles and their crews are visiting this planet from other planets."

World-renowned astrophysicist Stephen Hawking frequently expresses his belief in UFOs and extraterrestrials. The ETs avoid contact with us, he feels, because of our "instability" as a species and our warlike nature. "Of course it is possible that UFOs really do contain aliens as many people believe, and the government is hushing it up," he said in a recent television interview.

Incredibly, despite having no access to physical evidence confirming the existence of UFOs, the majority of Americans continue to believe that UFOs are real. In a 2002 Roper poll commissioned by television's *Sci-Fi Channel*, 56 percent of those surveyed said they believe UFOs are real. In addition, 72 percent of those polled believe that the U.S. government has not revealed everything it knows about UFOs. Thus, the issue of UFOs remains "a riddle, wrapped in a mystery, inside an enigma," to borrow a phrase from Winston Churchill.

It is within this context that we begin the narrative of the time when a flying saucer came blazing out of the sky and crashed a short distance from the U.S.-Mexico border near the tiny town of Coyame, Chihuahua. As the reader prepares for this bizarre journey down a hall of mirrors, our advice is to relax and enjoy the experience with an open mind. And, if it helps you to sleep better at night, you have our permission to regard the accounts in this book as pure flights of fancy.

Noe Torres
March 6, 2007

1. A STREAK IN THE NIGHT

The strangest of all things began with the dull routine of a hot summer evening at the United States Naval Air Station in Corpus Christi, Texas on Sunday, August 25, 1974. After a day in which temperatures soared to 87 degrees, activity at the naval base slowly wound down for the evening. By 9 p.m., the weather station at the base registered a temperature in the upper 70s with a six mile per hour breeze from the southeast blowing across the warm waters of the Gulf of Mexico.

As the weekend came to a close, some of the base personnel watched television, while others listened to their radios. Local baseball fans reveled in the news that the Houston Astros defeated the Philadelphia Phillies 5-0 in a game played earlier in the day at Houston's Astrodome, 150 miles north of Corpus Christi. On television, George Pal's celebrated 1953 science-fiction movie, *The War of the Worlds*, ran on a number of CBS affiliates.

In news of the day, Gerald R. Ford was settling in as President of the United States, after taking over on August 9 from the Watergate-troubled Richard Nixon. The *New York Times* announced that *Tinker, Tailor, Soldier, Spy* by John le Carre was number one on its weekly list of best selling novels. The *Los Angeles Times* Sunday edition spotlighted plans to set up an array of radio telescope antennas in New Mexico, designed to intercept radio signals from outer space. "Contact with other cultures could provide answers to many fascinating and fundamental questions," the article said.

A long way from Corpus Christi, ex-Beatle John Lennon was also wondering about contact with other worlds. He had called New York City police two days earlier, on August 23, claiming that he had seen a "flying saucer" from the terrace of his East Side apartment. Lennon's personal secretary, May Pang, later recalled, "He kept screaming for me to join him in that instant. As I walked out onto the terrace, my eye caught this large, circular object coming towards us. It was shaped like a flattened cone and on top was a large, brilliant red light...." Others also reported seeing a mysterious object in the skies over New York at about the same time.

Back in Corpus Christi, the subject of flying saucers was farthest from the minds of local residents. The largest city on the Texas Gulf Coast and the sixth largest port in the U.S., Corpus Christi had a 1974 population of about 280,000 people. The petroleum industry, the Naval Air Base, and local colleges and schools were the area's largest employers. Though it was one of the state's most populous cities, Corpus Christi in 1974 retained a close-knit small-town feel, heavily influenced by its largely Hispanic population. The city's claim to fame in the 1970s was that it was the hometown of Farah Fawcett-Majors, one of the most celebrated models and television actresses of the decade.

On August 25 at 10:00 p.m., Corpus Christi residents were turning in for the night, preparing themselves for the start of another workweek. One more warm summer night was upon them, and their cool, air-conditioned bedrooms beckoned.

At precisely 10:07 p.m. Central Daylight Time, the quiet radar screens at two different military installations along the Texas Gulf Coast lit up with the image of an unknown aircraft that suddenly appeared approximately 200 miles out in the Gulf of Mexico, headed inbound toward Corpus Christi. Radar operators watched in horror as the streaking object reached speeds of over 2,500 miles per hour while flying at an altitude of 75,000 feet, on a bearing of 325 degrees.

Air Defense Radar, Early 1980s (U.S. Dept. of Defense Photo)

Manmade jet aircraft of the time could barely make 2,200 mph and rarely flew above 50,000 feet. Therefore, an immediate concern was that the unidentified craft could be an enemy ballistic missile that had just dropped down out of the earth's atmosphere and was headed for Corpus Christi, one of the nation's key port cities.

If the strange object continued its course, it would intersect the Texas Gulf Coast about 40 miles south of Corpus Christi, in Kenedy County, just south of Baffin Bay. This rugged and isolated area of the state was the site of the monstrous ranching operation of the King Ranch, headquartered in nearby Kingsville.

Seconds after the object first appeared on radar, it moved to a position about 155 miles southeast of Corpus Christi. The radar image was monitored closely by Long Range Radar (LRR) at Ellington Air Force Base near Houston, Lackland Air Force Base in San Antonio, and the FAA radar facility in Oilton, Texas, all thee of which were part of U.S. Air Defense. Undoubtedly, radar operators at the Corpus Christi Naval Air Station and the Kingsville Naval Air Station also watched nervously as the unexpected night visitor moved on a course that would bring it over land in South Texas in a matter of moments.

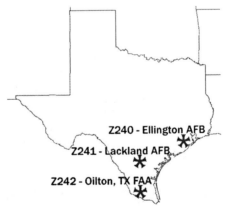

Map Showing Texas' Long Range Air Defense Radar Sites in the Early 1970s

How the object got so close to the Texas coast before being detected is unknown. When first painted by radar, it was already within 200 miles from Corpus Christi. That means it either descended into the skies above the Gulf of Mexico from outer space, or it came

10

up from below radar range and suddenly shot up to 75,000 feet. Most UFO researchers believe that the disk dropped down through the atmosphere from an orbit around our planet.

As radar observers continued to monitor its trajectory, the object suddenly slowed to about 1,950 miles per hour, simultaneously turned to a heading of 290 degrees, and began descending. To radar observers, the object's sudden and precise maneuvers indicated that it was being steered intelligently. Radar operators made a note that the object's new course would take the airship toward the southernmost tip of Texas, close to the city of Brownsville, another key Texas port city. Was this a missile that was now being diverted to another strategic U.S. target?

In the early stages of this sighting, some observers believed that the object might be a meteor because of its high speed and descending flight path. However, the sharp thirty-five degree change in direction and the controlled manner of descent quickly dispelled the notion that this was a meteor.

Given the object's strange behavior, U.S. air defense alerts were issued, and military jet fighters were prepped to intercept the object upon its entry into United States airspace. As military authorities along the Gulf Coast grew increasingly alarmed at the potentially dangerous situation, radar images continued to show the mysterious aircraft as it approached the Southern Gulf of Mexico, with a course that was trending south. The object was still descending.

Authors' Rendition of 8/25/74 Flying Disk

Brownsville, with its population of 52,000 people, sits right at the mouth of the Rio Grande River, and is the farthest point you can travel south and still be in the United States. On this strangest of nights in the summer of 1974, most residents of Brownsville were completely unaware of a strange glowing object tracing a line across the night sky southeast of the city. The unknown craft was easily within range of civilian radar at the small Brownsville airport, although no log entries were made about it. If spotters in Brownsville were tracking it, they were no doubt relieved when the object roared past them, still skirting the Texas coast and entering Mexican territorial waters.

At approximately 10:10 p.m., the luminous southbound streak suddenly veered to the west and entered Mexican airspace about forty miles south of Brownsville, along a desolate stretch of the northeastern coast of Mexico.

From an original altitude of 75,000 feet, the disk's altitude had gradually dropped and leveled off at 45,000 feet as it came over land in Mexico. It continued descending in a series of calculated, level steps, with each level of altitude being maintained for about five minutes. The intelligent, controlled descent was later described by co-author Ruben Uriarte to the *History Channel,* "This object was traveling and descending through steps, unlike that of a meteor which is more of an arc."

Traveling at close to 2,000 miles per hour while continuing to descend, the object moved to the west-northwest, a blazing fireball racing over the Mexican states of Tamaulipas, Nuevo Leon, Coahuila, and Chihuahua. UFO researchers point out that its course steered clear of major population centers from which military aircraft might be scrambled and missiles could be fired.

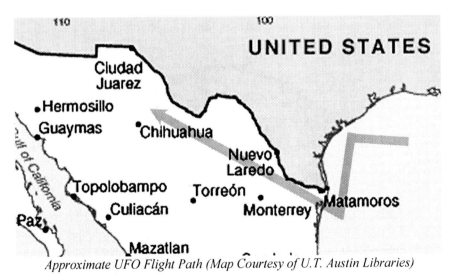

Approximate UFO Flight Path (Map Courtesy of U.T. Austin Libraries)

While the mysterious object maintained its course over sparsely populated wilderness areas of northern Mexico, U.S. military officials closely tracked the aircraft, worried that in a moment it could turn northward and cross the international boundary between Mexico and the United States. As it darted across northern Mexico, staying just south of the Rio Grande River, the flying disk came within radar range of the Air Force Base at Laredo, Texas, and was likely also picked up by radar at Laughlin Air Force Base, near Del Rio, Texas.

Traversing the skies over Coahuila state, the object, now moving northwest, zoomed past a very strange region of Mexico known as *La Zona del Silencio*, the Zone of Silence. Located about four hundred miles southeast of El Paso, the area got its name from the strange natural phenomena that have been observed there over the years. In addition to numerous sightings of UFOs and mysterious beings, the area is said to generate mysterious waves of electromagnetic energy that can disrupt radios, telephones, aircraft instruments, and other electronic devices.

It was over the northern part of this strange region that the unknown object of August 25, 1974 flew, as it streaked across Mexican airspace, seemingly avoiding the U.S. boundary. Within 30 minutes after it was first noticed on radar off the Corpus Christi coast, the object traveled 500 miles and was now blazing across the skies of the rugged and desolate Northern Mexican state of Chihuahua, within forty miles of the Texas border. Then something totally unexpected and unprecedented happened.

The strange craft that caused so much consternation and triggered such an intense concern on the part of the U.S. air defense network suddenly and mysteriously vanished from all radar screens. In a second, the blip on radar winked out of existence, leaving radar operators wondering if they had just seen a ghost.

Observers wondered if the object disappeared after dipping below the radar's horizon. Military officials continued to monitor radar screens, watching for signs that the object had re-emerged. When no such signs appeared after twenty minutes, the alert was cancelled, and plans to scramble military aircraft to intercept were abandoned.

But the story of the unidentified flying object that buzzed South Texas and disappeared near the Texas-Mexico border was just beginning....

2. THE PLANE CRASH

About half an hour before the strange object was first spotted on radar off the Texas coast, a small civilian aircraft took off from El Paso International Airport in El Paso, Texas. The takeoff was logged at approximately 9:30 p.m. on August 25, 1974. El Paso's temperature was in the mid 70s with 74 percent humidity, winds at six miles per hour, and visibility at 31 miles. Isolated thunderstorms in the area had produced less than a tenth of an inch of rain during the day. Sunset was 7:38 p.m. Mountain Time, with civil twilight ending at 8:03.

The small aircraft and its occupants, whose identities are unknown, headed southeast from El Paso quickly crossing the international boundary into the Mexican state of Chihuahua state. The small plane, believed to have been of Mexican registration, traveled at about 150 miles per hour and at an altitude somewhere between 3,000 and 7,000 feet, as it headed over the rugged mountain ranges of Northern Mexico.

Cessna Night Flight (Federal Aviation Administration)

About 200 miles southeast of El Paso, after a flight time just over an hour, the small plane flew over rugged mountainous terrain, moving south toward the sleepy Mexican village of Coyame, Chihuahua, within fifty miles of the Texas border. The plane's last reported position was about 100 miles northeast of Chihuahua City, one of Mexico's largest cities. Historical weather data shows that Chihuahua was experiencing temperatures in the mid 70s, humidity at 71 percent, visibility at 19 miles, and winds at 11 miles per hour.

14

Storms in the area had produced an inch of rain.

Just east of Coyame, across the Rio Grande River, is the Texas border town of Presidio, a small community of about 2,000 residents and one of the oldest settlements in the United States. Presidio is in an area of Texas that has long been associated with mystery and the supernatural.

Near Presidio are the Chinati Mountains of West Texas, which for many years have been the setting for strange, unexplained flickering lights whose origins remain unknown to this day. From the nearby town of Marfa, observers looking back south toward the 7,728-foot Chinati Peak often see strange colored lights that randomly appear and disappear among the mountain peaks. These so-called *Marfa Lights*, which some people believe are UFOs, have been seen in this region since the time of its earliest settlers.

Within ten miles farther north is the eerie, isolated "ghost" town of Shafter, Texas, where parts of the landmark science-fiction movie *The Andromeda Strain* were filmed. In the 1971 movie, based on a novel by Michael Crichton, an object from space that crashes in a small town and unleashes a lethal extraterrestrial virus that scientists fear will soon engulf the entire planet. Among the actions taken to contain the virus, the U.S. military obliterates the town using a low-yield nuclear device. Critics praised the film for accurately describing how U.S. authorities might actually respond to an extraterrestrial biological infestation.

It is indeed a remote and mysterious area of North America near which the flight of the small airplane ended on August 25, 1974. Sometime around 10:30 p.m., the plane suddenly disappeared from radar screens and was presumed to have gone down in the vicinity of Coyame, Chihuahua.

Arrow Marks Crash Site (Map Courtesy of U.T. Austin Libraries)

15

At about 11:00 p.m., persons monitoring civilian radio traffic in the area heard a report that a small aircraft had crashed near Coyame. Word quickly reached military officials in nearby Chihuahua and Ojinaga, and plans were set in motion for a search and rescue operation to begin at daybreak. A search of this remote, rugged landscape in the darkness of night would certainly prove fruitless. As far as anyone knew at this point, the incident was simply a crash of a small airplane carrying one or two persons into the jagged mountain peaks of northern Mexico.

Interestingly though, the private aircraft disappeared from radar at the exact time that radar contact was lost with another aircraft flying in the same area. That other craft was the strange object that traveled across the Gulf of Mexico and into Northern Mexico before vanishing without a trace. It was only a matter of time before investigators concluded that the two aircraft had collided somewhere over the mountains around Coyame. The crash took place at an altitude of between 3,000 and 7,000 feet, with the small plane traveling south-southeast at about 150 mph and the UFO traveling west-northwest at close to 2,000 mph.

Artistic Representation of the Aircraft About to Crash (Juarez OVNI Group)

Co-author Ruben Uriarte believes that a factor in the crash was the presence of the many rocky mountain peaks that rise up all around the area of the accident. Uriarte said, "What I found fascinating was that the crash may have been caused by both craft colliding at a lower altitude due to their vision being blocked by a high peak, hills, or mountain. In other words, both craft met at an intersection of the mountain. If the plane was flying south and the craft was flying west, the pilot couldn't have seen anything on his left until he cleared the mountain, colliding with the craft in front of him. In addition to this, the darkness of night was another key factor."

Uriarte gives the example of a vehicle approaching an intersection where the driver's vision is blocked by a large building located immediately to his left. As he is completely blind to any traffic coming from the left, if he proceeds into the intersection, there is always a chance of a collision. In addition, Uriarte says, the airplane pilot may have been temporarily distracted or may have suffered an instrument malfunction. Blinded by the surrounding peaks, some of which tower close to 5,000 feet, the two aircraft came to a sudden and unexpected union. The two blips on radar screens suddenly became one and then disappeared.

The Vast Plain Known as "El Llano," Located North of Coyame (2007 by Ruben Uriarte)

Both aircraft spiraled out of control and crashed in the rugged desert below. As military officials on the north side of the Rio Grande River started putting the radar evidence together, they became convinced that the unidentified flying object that lit up military radar screens and caused the U.S. air defense network to go into alert mode was now on the ground. It was lying somewhere amid miles of rocks, cacti, chaparral, and agaves in a mountainous region near of Coyame, Chihuahua, Mexico.

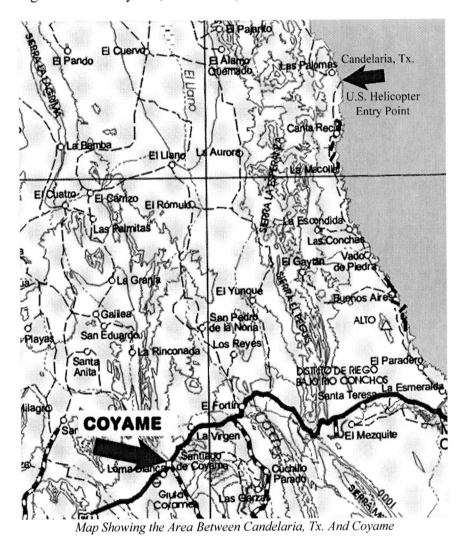

Map Showing the Area Between Candelaria, Tx. And Coyame

Because the U.S. helicopters that recovered the crashed disk entered Mexico at a point just north of Candelaria, Texas, UFO researchers believe that the recovery site was in the desert immediately west of Candelaria and just north of Coyame. Among those who believe that this vast, rugged ranching country is where the 1974 crash occurred is Gilberto E. Rivera Altamirano, director of GIFAE (Group for the Investigation of Aerial Phenomena) in Chihuahua City. A vast flat plain called *El Llano* dominates the area of the suspected crash location. One would be hard pressed to find a more desolate rocky wilderness in all of northern Mexico. As in other UFO cases, this event became closely associated with the name of the largest town in the area, although the crash site is estimated to have been perhaps as much as 50 air miles away from the actual town of Coyame.

This is an area of extreme desolation and mystery, according to Jorge A. González Almeida, a Chihuahua City attorney, who has been a frequent visitor to the area since his childhood and owns almost 30,000 acres of desert land northeast of Coyame. "I have spent a lot of time, since my youth, hunting in this land," González explains, "And I have seen a lot of strange, unexplained things in the skies above the ranches." In an exclusive interview for this book, González told the authors, "I personally have witnessed numerous unexplained phenomena in this area, and I have also heard many stories from others."

Terrain North of Coyame (Courtesy of Jorge A. González Almeida)

19

"The mountains in this region are rich in uranium," González says. "The local people say that the abundance of uranium sometimes causes these strange glowing lights and other phenomena, but I personally don't think it's the uranium." Interestingly, many UFO sightings over the years have been reported in and around uranium-rich areas all around the world, including South America, Africa, Europe, and the United States.

A recent report of the Geological Society of America states, "Uranium prospects were developed during the early 1960s in limestone and alluvium at the internal drainage basins of Chihuahua. More than 100 wells were drilled along the eastern side of the Sierra del Cuervo. The drilled wells in alluvium cover an area of 60 by 2 km. The first economic findings were made in limestone, but later more than 100 radiometric anomalies were identified in igneous rocks.... Uranium exploration continued in the 1970s at other sites in Chihuahua. By 1980 several findings made it possible to interpret the origin of uranium-mineralizing fluids in the Peña Blanca Uranium District... This work is being revised now because high alpha radioactivity has been detected in water of Chihuahua City."

The area around Coyame is strange indeed. And, although Mexico's Federal Highway 16, built in 1992, now offers a smooth paved ride between the International Bridge at Ojinaga and Chihuahua City, visitors to this area still feel an eerie isolation and sense of foreboding. Despite the presence of the highway, Coyame nonetheless gives the impression of being well off the beaten path. This was especially true in 1974, before the present highway was built, and it is certainly true of the ranches located in the rugged mountainous areas north of Coyame.

Given their relative isolation and mostly uneventful history, the local residents had little reason to suspect that their area was about to become the focal point of an event of staggering proportions. Little did they realize that on that warm August night in 1974, this isolated region was about to move front and center in an amazing race between two governments to recover extraterrestrial technology from a crashed spaceship.

3. CRASH SITE

Because the crash of the two aircraft occurred in the dark of night along a rugged stretch of the Chihuahuan Desert far from the nearest town of any size, no attempts were made to locate the wreckage until the following morning -- Monday, August 26, 1974. As U.S. authorities analyzed the radar data from the night before and began to suspect that the unidentified flying object they had tracked did in fact collide with the private airplane, Mexican aviation officials mounted a search near Coyame. Since the plane was registered in Mexico and the crash occurred in Mexico, it was clearly their case, despite the flight having originated in El Paso.

At 8:00 a.m., some nine hours after the small plane disappeared in the skies near Coyame, the Mexican rescue effort began. As dawn broke over the area, a spotter plane circled the mountainous region around Coyame, looking for evidence of wreckage. The plane was most likely dispatched from Chihuahua City, 100 miles to the southwest. With a population close to half a million inhabitants, Chihuahua City is home to two major bases of the *Fuerza Aerea Mexicana* (Mexican Air Force). Although the Mexican military may not yet have been aware of the reported crash of an unidentified flying object, they clearly knew that a small aircraft bound from El Paso to Mexico City had gone down somewhere north of Coyame, in the midst of a wide expanse of rugged ranchland. The troops were most likely summoned from the Mexican army base in nearby Ojinaga.

El Paso Electronic Surveillance Center (U.S. Border Patrol)

Unknown to the Mexicans involved in the rescue effort, electronic surveillance from across the Rio Grande River was closely monitoring all their moves and all radio communications regarding the attempt to locate the downed aircraft. The events of the night before and the possibility of a crashed extraterrestrial airship had brought America's considerable intelligence resources to bear in the scrutiny of what appeared on the surface to merely be an attempt to find a small plane that crashed in the Mexican desert nine hours earlier.

Significant U.S. military intelligence gathering assets were available at Fort Bliss, a mammoth U.S. Army base at El Paso, Texas. Fort Bliss had been the home of sophisticated electronic information gathering efforts since at least the early 1970s. Established at the base in 1974, the El Paso Intelligence Center (EPIC) was assigned the task of monitoring the U.S.-Mexico border as part of the effort to stem the flow of illegal drugs and immigrants into the United States.

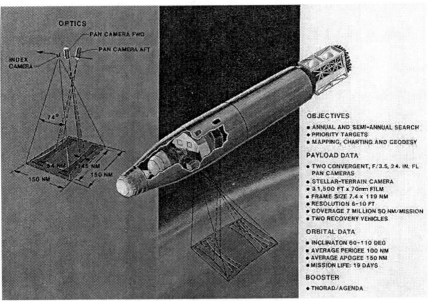

Diagram of U.S. Spy Satellite (NRO)

Another available surveillance resource for the U.S. military was its fleet of Keyhole KH-9 spy satellites, known as "Big Birds." First put into orbit in 1971, the Keyholes eventually numbered twenty and were capable of focusing in on an object on the ground as small as six inches. Flying at altitudes between 175 and 625 miles above the earth, the KH-9 satellites used conventional cameras to capture thousands of photographs in four huge film canisters, which were then ejected down to the earth for retrieval by U.S. authorities.

Also, U.S. military planes were also available to fly over the Coyame crash site to take photographs and capture data. The EP-3E Aries I electronic surveillance aircraft, which entered service in 1971, was in the military's repertoire and available for use in the Coyame surveillance. Also available were military jets originating from Fort Bliss or from the Air Force bases in Del Rio and Laredo.

Sometime during the nighttime hours of August 25, 1974, the site of a seemingly routine aircraft crash about thirty miles from the Texas border had suddenly blossomed into a global intelligence hotspot that was starting to draw more and more of America's military surveillance assets.

Beginning at about 8:00 a.m. on August 26, the electronic listening assets began picking up radio traffic from the Mexican military personnel who were flying over Coyame looking for the site of the small airplane crash. At 10:30 a.m., amidst the crackle of the faint Mexican radio signals, U.S. listeners heard a Mexican military pilot report that he spotted from the air signs of a wrecked aircraft in the desert near Coyame. The crashed plane was characterized as having been "almost totally destroyed."

So far, this was a routine airplane crash investigation. The wreckage of the Mexico City-bound civilian aircraft had been found. The Mexicans would likely next assemble a team to visit the site, search for survivors, and inspect the wreckage. To the anxious listeners north of the Rio Grande River, nothing had been said to arouse any further interest on their part.

Suddenly, the radio crackled again with a message from the Mexican pilot about a second downed "plane" only a few miles from the first wreckage. Whereas only scattered debris remained of the small airplane, the second craft was described as being nearly intact and circular in shape with a silver metallic finish that glinted in the hot Mexican sun. The pilot noted that the gleaming disk showed some signs of superficial damage but that it was still "in one piece."

23

The stunning news on the intercepted radio transmission caused a sudden flurry of activity on the U.S. side of the border, as military personnel rushed to inform their supervisors of the Mexican discovery. Plans were quickly drawn up to bring more surveillance assets to bear on the Coyame crash and also to prepare a U.S. military team for rapid deployment into Mexico to recover the mysterious disk.

U.S. hopes for a continued stream of information from Mexican radio intercepts were quickly dashed. Shortly after the Mexican pilot's statement that he had found a second crash site, a voice came on the radio to announce that a radio silence was in effect. No further discussion about the discovery of the crash sites was permitted on the airwaves.

Despite the loss of Mexican radio transmissions, the gears of the U.S. military and intelligence machinery were already in motion. From the electronic surveillance center at El Paso's Fort Bliss, the message about the crashed UFO was undoubtedly quickly passed to the Central Intelligence Agency, which immediately became involved in the matter.

CIA Headquarters at Langley, Virginia, Circa 1974 (CIA Photo)

Shortly after the call came in to CIA Headquarters at Langley, Virginia, CIA Director William Colby may have contacted newly appointed U.S. President Gerald R. Ford to apprise him of the rapidly developing situation along the Texas-Mexico border. Not one to shy away from the topic of UFOs, President Ford, when he was majority leader in the U.S. Congress in 1966, said, "I believe Congress should thoroughly investigate the rash of reported sightings of unidentified flying objects in Southern Michigan and other parts of the country. I feel a Congressional inquiry would be most worthwhile because the American people are intensely interested in the UFO stories, and some people are alarmed by them."

Ford's eagerness to investigate UFOs vanished inexplicably after he assumed the presidency in August of 1974. UFO enthusiasts have speculated that certain key intelligence officials may have conspired to keep UFO information away from the President Ford. Others claim that, in the wake of evidence such as that gathered in the 1974 Coyame crash, the president may have changed his viewpoint and joined those who believe it is in society's best interest to keep UFO truths hidden.

President Ford, Circa 1974 (Gerald R. Ford Presidential Library)

In any event, the reported crash of a UFO near Coyame, Chihuahua sent shockwaves through the U.S. intelligence community, and within hours after the Mexican radio transmission was intercepted, Central Intelligence Agency operatives were at Fort Bliss in El Paso, busily assembling a UFO recovery team. The team's stealthy mission was to make a rapid entry into the territory of a foreign country to recover, if possible, the artifacts of a crashed extraterrestrial spacecraft.

It is possible that U.S. intelligence agencies maintain rapid-deploy recovery teams ever "on the ready" for quick missions such as the Coyame crash retrieval. UFO researcher Elaine Douglass, before the Coyame event became public, interviewed a soldier in Washington, D.C. who told her he served on a number of these rapid strike missions. Douglass said, "He made it plain that recovering extraterrestrial physical evidence was one of types of missions that his team and other teams like it were prepared to undertake and had undertaken."

Unlike the 1947 UFO crash near Roswell, New Mexico, which took place when the U.S. intelligence community was in its infancy, the Coyame crash occurred after the intelligence agencies were seasoned by many years of Cold War experience and by the Korean and Vietnam Wars. By 1974, the United States had the military and intelligence wherewithal to quickly and efficiently respond to an incident like the Coyame crash.

4. THE MEXICAN RECOVERY TEAM

Early in the afternoon of Monday, August 26, 1974, a convoy of Mexican military vehicles, operating under strict radio silence, made its way across the harsh Chihuahuan desert near Coyame toward the crash sites of the two aircraft. Shortly after the spotter plane's discovery, the convoy rumbled out of Ojinaga, about 60 miles away, with up to 24 soldiers and vehicles that included several large flatbed trucks with winches and a number of jeeps. The convoy headed west along the Ojinaga-Chihuahua highway but then turned north into the desert some 20 miles before reaching Coyame, probably in the vicinity of El Fortín. Once in the desert, the soldiers could follow a well-marked system of dirt roads enabling them to easily reach their destination and then continue on all the way to Chihuahua, if that was where they had been instructed to go after making the retrieval.

U.S. government officials, worried that they were quickly losing their chance to learn more about the strange object that crashed in the Mexican desert, contacted their counterparts in the Mexican government, requesting permission to "assist" with the recovery of the wreckage. An anonymous source later said that communication between the two governments was held "at the highest levels," as the U.S. argued that it should be involved in the recovery effort because the crashed civilian aircraft had departed from U.S. soil. It is also possible that the U.S. told the Mexicans that the unknown aircraft had caused an alert of U.S. air defense systems prior to its disappearance near Coyame.

According to the anonymous U.S. source that later disclosed the essential information about this case, the Mexican government was hesitant to allow U.S. involvement early in the recovery operation. Further, the Mexicans insisted that they knew nothing about a second airship and stated that their operation was simply a routine recovery of a crashed plane. As high-level communications between the two governments continued on August 26, Mexican authorities held firm that they did not need any assistance from the U.S. government.

The Mexicans followed a historical pattern of behavior that had been established during a number of previous crashes of U.S. test missiles (and possibly UFOs) in Northern Mexico. The Mexican military typically conducted the search, controlled the crash site, sifted through the debris looking for anything of interest, and then eventually allowed U.S. recovery teams to enter the area. This pattern emerged during V-2 missile crashes near El Paso in the late 1940s and extended into the 1970s, including the July 11, 1970 crash of an Athena intercontinental ballistic test missile near Durango, Coahuila, Mexico.

On this August afternoon in 1974, even as the U.S. continued to offer to assist the Mexicans, the military convoy finally arrived at the desert location near Coyame where the two aircraft crashed. The Mexican team probably first visited the debris field from the crash of the small airplane. The soldiers quickly gathered up the pieces of the wrecked plane and placed them on one or more of their trucks. Earlier radio transmissions had described the small plane as "almost totally destroyed," and there were few large pieces remaining. Body parts, if found, were zipped up in body bags and added to the trucks' cargo.

The convoy then moved to the second crash site, a few miles away, where the astonished soldiers witnessed a site that none of them could have prepared for. Walking slowly across the rocky desert terrain, the soldiers carefully approached a shiny metal disk impacted into the ground. The disk measured sixteen feet, five inches, in diameter and slightly less than five feet from top to bottom.

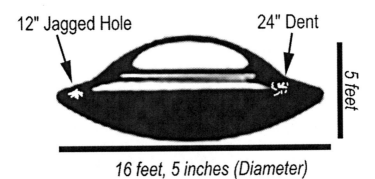

12" Jagged Hole   **24" Dent**

5 feet

16 feet, 5 inches (Diameter)

Authors' Rendition of Coyame UFO

As the Mexican soldiers walked around the object, they further noticed that it was equally convex on both the upper and lower surfaces, and there were no doors, windows, lights, or evident means of propulsion. It was simply a smooth, silver-colored aerodynamic "classic" flying saucer shape, silver in color, with the appearance of polished steel.

Further investigation revealed no markings of any kind on the craft. Around the outer "rim" of the saucer, the soldiers noticed two areas of damage to the ship. One was an irregular hole, approximately 12 inches in diameter, with the material around the hole being caved inward. The other damage point along the rim was simply a two-foot-wide dent in the shiny metal surface.

The 12-inch hole in the otherwise sealed exterior of the spacecraft is of particular note. In retrospect, this cavity might have been viewed with a wary eye, for out of it could be expelled extraterrestrial contaminants from within the ship into the environment surrounding the exterior. Although no visible venting was noted during the soldiers' cursory examination, later events suggested that something invisible to the human eye was being vented from the craft, most likely from out of this breach in the outer metallic shell of the structure.

Artist's Rendition of Mexican Soldier Looking at Crashed Disk (Juarez OVNI Group)

All during the time that the Mexican recovery team was busy attaching straps to the crashed saucer and hoisting it onto the bed of one of their trucks, an unknown contaminant was working on the men. Wearing no form of protective suits, masks, or gloves, the entire Mexican team was fully exposed to the mysterious agent.

Over the course of the late morning and early afternoon, as the Mexicans worked on recovering the wreckage from both crash sites, U.S. military aircraft flying at high altitude recorded observations and took photographs of the Mexican team's progress. A U.S. spy satellite, probably a Keyhole KH-9, was retasked to also take photos from orbit of the Mexican salvage operation. As the hot summer afternoon wore on, the U.S. reconnaissance assets showed that the Mexicans had succeeded in recovering all the wreckage from both crash sites and had placed each site's wreckage on a separate flatbed truck, covered by canvas.

With the wreckage safely stowed on the trucks, the convoy proceeded across the desert in a southerly directly toward Chihuahua City. For the U.S. intelligence officials watching from north of the Rio Grande River, their opportunity to intercede and gain access to the extraterrestrial artifacts was quickly slipping away.

5. THE U.S. RECOVERY TEAM

On the morning of August 26, 1974, CIA officials listened in anxious silence to the reports coming out of Mexico. From the radar data of the night before to the static-filled Mexican radio transmission about a second crash site, the chain of evidence quickly escalated the concern among U.S. intelligence officials. The CIA entered the situation early on, with several other federal agencies and the military providing them with logistical support.

Immediately upon hearing that the Mexicans had found a crashed UFO, the CIA ordered a gathering of men and materiel deep within the massive Fort Bliss Military Reservation for a rapid response task force whose mission was to enter Mexico quickly and recover the alien disk. The rapidity with which this team assembled is staggering. The team was operationally ready to deploy by noon on August 26, less than two hours after the intercepted Mexican radio transmission about the second crash site.

The team's rapid deployment seems to fit the theory that teams such as this were already in place and on "stand by" awaiting orders. At the very least, the team was operating on a carefully pre-planned script that had already been carefully mapped out. It took an amazingly short time to bring together highly specialized personnel, equipment, supplies, and air vehicles from all over the country. The speed with which this happened argues for the existence of a "playbook," or precise formula. The UFO crash recovery operation moved flawlessly through a logical series of meticulously planned and prepared steps that immediately brought into play a number of critical U.S. military and intelligence assets, gathered from every corner of the nation.

The sprawling Fort Bliss military reservation provided the perfect staging ground for this clandestine excursion into Mexico. One of the largest Army posts in the country, Fort Bliss encompasses 1,119,700 acres. Although the main post and headquarters buildings are located near downtown El Paso, the military reservation extends for many miles beyond the Texas state line and well into New Mexico, where it adjoins the territory of the

White Sands Missile Range.

Within the boundaries of this huge compound, the military conducts artillery training, tank maneuvers, Patriot missile test launches, and ground forces training. As of 2005, Fort Bliss employed about 23,000 military and civilian personnel.

Fort Bliss (arrow) and Adjoining Military Lands (NationalAtlas.gov)

On August 26, 1974, in a highly secure area of Fort Bliss where the public is never allowed, four helicopters landed and underwent preparation for the UFO recovery mission. Based on eyewitness accounts, three of the helicopters were probably Bell UH-1 Hueys, configured for special operations, and one of them was a much larger bird, possibly a Sikorsky CH-53D Sea Stallion, a so-called "Giant Helicopter."

The UH-1 Iroquis series "Hueys," used extensively in Vietnam, are flown by a crew of two and can accommodate up to 13 passengers. They fly at up to 140 mph at a maximum functional altitude of 10,000 feet. Whereas the larger helicopter would be the workhorse of the Coyame mission, the Hueys would provide extremely rapid deployment, firepower, and additional personnel transport capabilities.

UH-1 Huey Gunship (U.S. Army Photo)

The Sikorsky CH-53D heavy-lift Sea Stallion helicopter, capable of carrying up to seven tons worth of cargo, would be used to transport the recovered wreckage back to the United States. Accommodating up to 55 passengers, the Sea Stallion would also carry additional equipment, supplies, and personnel.

The four helicopters being prepped in a secret corner of the Fort Bliss reservation did not look like standard military aircraft. They carried no markings or logos of any kind that would have identified them as belonging to any United States military branch or federal agency. They were painted a neutral sand color, presumably to blend more easily into a Chihuahuan Desert landscape.

While final preparations were made on the helicopters, including the loading of all equipment and supplies for the mission, the helicopter crews remained with their aircraft and had absolutely no contact with any of the Fort Bliss personnel who were helping with the pre-flight logistics. The helicopter crews were obviously under strict orders to keep to themselves and reveal no information to anyone about the mission for which they had been briefed.

Less than two hours after the Mexican military spotted the second crash site near Coyame, the CIA's rapid deployment UFO recovery team was fully operational and awaiting the order to "go." Among the personnel standing by to board the helicopters and commence the mission was a team of individuals specially trained for assessing and handling a scene involving extraterrestrial artifacts. Included in the team were members with significant scientific and medical training.

Sikorsky CH-53D Sea Stallions (U.S. Navy Photo)

While the team's deployment preparations were being made, the mission's decision makers, located elsewhere in a heavy-secured section of Fort Bliss, examined the latest photographs from satellite and reconnaissance aircraft. They saw that by late afternoon, the Mexican recovery team had already loaded the wreckage from both crash sites onto their trucks and was proceeding away from the area, headed south toward Chihuahua City. The U.S. officials saw that their objective was escaping them, and soon the game would be up. The time for a go-or-no-go decision was rapidly approaching.

Then an amazing thing happened that changed everything and made a green-light decision much easier. Another set of reconnaissance photographs showed that the Mexican convoy had stopped dead in its tracks in the middle of the desert and had not moved from its position in the previous set of photographs. The line of convoy vehicles had managed to travel some distance from the UFO crash site, but clearly the vehicles were no longer moving. The convoy's progress had come to a standstill in a rugged area, still far from any major roads or populated areas. U.S. officials struggled to understand what might have stopped the Mexicans. Unfortunately, the high-altitude flyovers and satellite imagery were not enough to explain what happened.

The decision makers at Fort Bliss ordered that a military reconnaissance jet be sent out immediately on a low-altitude, high-speed flight over the Mexican military convoy's position. Given the aircraft available in 1974, they possibly dispatched a North American RA-5C "Vigilante," a McDonnell-Douglas RF-4C "Phantom II," or a Vought RF-8G "Crusader," each of which saw significant reconnaissance duty in Vietnam. Since these aircraft travel at over 1,200 mph, each could make the 200-air-mile trip from El Paso to Coyame in ten minutes. If the aircraft launched from another airbase in Texas, the travel time would increase only slightly.

The detailed photographs returned to Fort Bliss from the low-altitude flyover depicted a horrifying scene from the Mexican desert. The pictures again showed the line of vehicles making up the Mexican convoy, but this closer view showed why the vehicles were no longer moving. Several vehicle doors had been thrown wide open, and two human bodies lay in the sand beside two of the vehicles. There was no sign of any living person, and the assumption was that the other members of the Mexican recovery team were dead or dying inside the other vehicles.

To the mission leaders at Fort Bliss, no other decision could be made but to immediately send their team to Coyame and recover the artifacts and neutralize any possible threat to the U.S. border only thirty miles away. Clearly, the tactical situation had changed. A lethal agent had been introduced into the mix. Something had killed the unsuspecting Mexican soldiers within a couple of hours of exposure. The causal agent could be chemical, biological, radiological, or something totally unknown. As the Mexicans were apparently not aware that they had been exposed, the killer was certainly invisible and caused no symptoms until the very end.

Prior to finally launching the U.S. recovery mission, U.S. officials may have informed the Mexican government that they were going in. This communiqué may have occurred at very high levels of government, during which the Americans may have emphasized the extreme peril of the contamination that the Mexican soldiers had unleashed.

It is possible that, given the frightening specter of an unknown lethal contaminant so close to the border, the Mexican government, while not granting permission, decided that it would not protest the incursion by the U.S. task force. UFO researcher B.J. Booth thinks the Americans decided they were moving in, regardless of whether Mexico cleared it or not. Booth says, "They can always find a way to enter foreign territory and justify it with the American people. However, dealing with the Mexican government would have necessitated them using the ploy of assistance and life saving helping hands to go into Mexico."

The order to send the UFO recovery team was officially given but then delayed pending the arrival of more equipment and two additional team members. Since the team had previously already been declared operationally ready, the decision to wait for these extra assets to arrive suggests that additional safeguards and procedures had to be put into place at the last minute in view of the presence of a lethal agent at the Mexican convoy site.

The delay in departure served one more key purpose. It allowed the U. S. team to acquire the tools it needed to assist in carrying out its mission and, if necessary, "disinfecting" the scene of the contamination. A likely last-minute addition to the recovery team's manifest was an MK-54 Special Atomic Demolition Munition (SADM), the U.S. military's infamous "suitcase nuke" that was developed in the early 1960s and was present in the arsenal until the 1980s.

As a low-yield, easily transportable nuclear device, the SADM might be easily mistaken for a pack of conventional high explosives. With a minimum yield equivalent to ten tons of TNT, the SADM provided a lethally effective method of cleansing an area of biological contaminants. The small nuclear blast would virtually eliminate the chance that the contaminants would be dispersed over a wide area, as might happen with conventional explosives.

At 2:38 p.m. on Monday, August 26, with the extra equipment and personnel aboard, the convoy of helicopters lifted off from the secret location in the Fort Bliss military reservation, headed southeast along the Texas-Mexico border toward the small town of Candelaria, Texas, about 150 air miles away. The exact number of persons traveling in the four helicopters is unknown, but estimates range from 20-50.

Obviously, an early objective was to remain on the U.S. side of the international border for as long as possible so as not to arouse any suspicion from ground observers in Mexico. The flight along the north side of the Rio Grande River from El Paso to Candelaria took the helicopters over one of the most desolate areas of Texas. There are no major roads or population centers along this mountainous stretch, which encompasses the Quitman Mountains and the Sierra Vieja Mountains, among other ranges. Except where the helicopter convoy flew over a small segment of Interstate 10 in Hudspeth County, southeast of El Paso, this flight path offered the most stealth, thereby raising the fewest questions among local inhabitants.

As they approached Candelaria from the north, the unmarked helicopters suddenly veered across the Rio Grande River, penetrating Mexican airspace. Using the surrounding mountain ranges as cover, they continued an additional 50 to 70 miles, finally arriving at the scene of the Mexican military convoy somewhere near Coyame. Because the helicopter team veered into Mexico at a point approximately 53 air miles northeast of Coyame, the crash recovery site is generally believed to have been north or northeast of Coyame, perhaps in a large flat plain called *El Llano*. Time was of the essence, as the Americans were determined to put a stop to what seemed to be a serious threat to all human life in the region.

Whatever contaminant the Mexicans had unloosed from the alien ship was a mere thirty miles from the United States, and if borne across the border by air, the result might be apocalyptic. It was with a deepening sense of the importance of their mission that the team members sat quietly in their harnesses waiting to arrive in a place that was full of both earthly and otherworldly danger. The earthly peril lay in being discovered by the Mexican military. The otherworldly danger was in being exposed to a lethal agent of extraterrestrial origin. Daniel was indeed being delivered into the lion's den.

As the team approached its destination in the Mexican desert, word was passed to all team members to don their chemical protective equipment (CPE). If a lethal contaminant was still present in the area, it could begin to affect them at any moment once they approached the scene. The CPE gear offered team members head-to-toe protection against a variety of chemical and biological toxic agents. Each person's equipment included: a field protective hood and mask, a protective overgarment, vinyl overboots, and protective gloves.

Soldier in Chemical Protective Gear (U.S. Army Photo)

6. "They're All Dead!"

At 4:53 p.m. on Monday, August 26, just slightly more than two hours after departing Fort Bliss, the rapid-deploy UFO recovery team arrived over the stretch of Chihuahuan Desert where the Mexican convoy vehicles had stopped moving. As the helicopters surveyed the area before landing, the team members were struck by terror at what they saw. The line of Mexican military jeeps and trucks looked as if it had been frozen in time. There was absolutely no movement. As shown in the reconnaissance photos, several vehicles had their doors ajar, and the bodies of two soldiers were sprawled on the desert sand near the open doors of their jeeps.

Terrain Around Coyame (Courtesy of Jorge A. González Almeida)

Slowly and deliberately, the four unmarked helicopters touched down on the desert floor a short distance away from the lead vehicle of the Mexican convoy. Moments later, dressed in full protective gear, the team members exited their aircraft and moved out to execute their carefully planned mission to recover extraterrestrial technological artifacts, neutralize any contamination, and eliminate all traces of the alien ship's crash. Another part of the team, selected to provide security against any persons approaching the area while the mission was ongoing, fanned out, weapons drawn, to form a defense perimeter. Possibly, another part of the team began preparations for deployment of a low-yield nuclear device to be used after the team had finished its work at the site.

A preliminary visual inspection of the scene found that all of the members of the Mexican recovery team were in fact already dead. Most of them were found slumped over inside the convoy's trucks. The cause of death was not immediately evident.

The original report of this case said, "Unfortunately what caused the deaths of the Mexican recovery team is not known. Speculation ranges from a chemical released from the [UFO] as a result of the damage, to a microbiological agent. There are no indications of death or illness by any of the [U.S.] recovery team. It would not have been illogical for the recovery team to have taken one of the bodies back with them for analysis. But there is no indication of that having happen. Perhaps they did not have adequate means of transporting what might have been a biologically contaminated body."

Certain of the team's personnel carried out the grim task of removing all of the bodies and loading them onto the bed of one of the Mexican trucks. Another part of the team quickly located the truck carrying the alien spacecraft, which had been strapped to the bed of one of the trucks and covered by a large tarp. The airship was examined very quickly, while the rest of the team conducted other phases of the mission. Several quick field tests were undoubtedly conducted, designed to detect various chemical and biological agents in the surrounding environment. There simply was no time for anything beyond these most cursory of tests.

Fearing that Mexican reinforcements could arrive on the scene at any time, team members began to prep the crashed disk for transport via the CH-53D Sea Stallion. Since the spaceship had to be carried back to the United States while suspended from the large helicopter's cargo cable, the team had two critical steps to take in preparing for transport. First, team members had seal the outer surface of the alien craft with a protective covering to guard against any further venting of lethal agents during the transport. Exactly what type of covering was used is unknown; however, the military had at its disposal materials developed by NASA for covering a returning Apollo moon capsule in the event of an accident during re-entry.

After the crashed saucer was wrapped, the recovery team had to ensure that while being transported to the U.S. it could not be identified by curious spectators on the ground. Therefore, they completely covered the ship using a tarp to camouflage it.

These steps having been accomplished, the straps that the Mexicans had used to secure it to their truck were reconfigured for attaching them to the Sea Stallion's cargo cable. The pilot of the giant helicopter then positioned his aircraft directly over the extraterrestrial ship and waited as the soldiers down below attached the cable. The mysterious object's weight was later estimated at 1,500 pounds, which was no problem at all for the Sea Stallion, which is capable of carrying cargo exceeding 30,000 pounds.

At exactly 5:14 p.m., a mere 21 minutes after the team first landed in the desert, the UFO was lifted into the air and quickly borne away to the east over the rugged peaks of the neighboring mountains. Although a major part of the mission was now complete, the remaining team members were still engaged in a flurry of activity.

After the Sea Stallion's departure, soldiers finished loading all the bodies onto the Mexican trucks. Apparently no effort was made by any team members to conduct an investigation in the field into the cause of death. There is also no record of any of the bodies having been taken back to the U.S. for analysis. It is possible that no such efforts were made due to the pressures of time from being an uninvited military force on a foreign country's soil. Or perhaps the operational procedures for this type of mission did not include removal of lethally contaminated bodies. UFO researcher Elaine Douglass was told by a former member of a similar rapid-deploy recovery team that his unit was under specific orders not to retrieve any bodies found at the scene.

Some researchers speculate that the actions of the U.S. team indicate a prior knowledge of the properties and characteristics of the lethal agent that killed the Mexicans. Perhaps this substance had been encountered before, and there was no pressing need to investigate it in this instance. Perhaps the mechanism of death was discovered shortly after the U.S. team arrived.

As their final act before leaving, the remaining team members drove all of the Mexican vehicles together to form as tight a formation as they could. Within the group of vehicles were the trucks containing the debris from the crash of the civilian aircraft that had struck the UFO, as well as the bodies of all of the Mexican soldiers.

What happened next, although it might seem shocking, is understandable in terms of the danger posed by lethal contagion from the dead bodies. The original account of these events states that all the Mexican vehicles and bodies were destroyed with "high explosives." As the writer of that account was likely not a munitions expert, what he described as "high explosives" could have been an MK-54 Special Atomic Demolition Munition, which had been available to the U.S. military since the early 1960s.

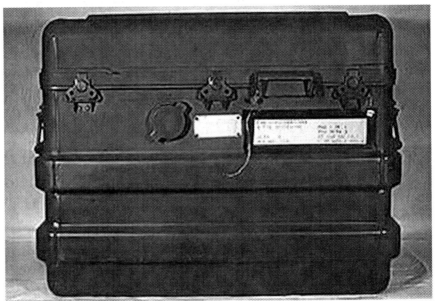

MK-54 SADM "Suitcase Nuke"(U.S. Military Photo)

The SADM was a variation of a nuclear device that was labeled "W54" when the Los Alamos Scientific Laboratory designed it in the late 1950s. The W54 was the smallest nuclear warhead ever

42

deployed by the United States. An implosion type Plutonium bomb, the W54 could deliver a variable yield that could be configured for anywhere between 10 tons and 1 kiloton. The smallest yield, 10 tons, would have affected a very small area of the surrounding desert, leaving virtually no residual effects. This was likely the setting used to "cleanse" the convoy site, as it would have the least impact on nearby populations and natural resources. The device was trigged by the use of a mechanical timer.

B.J. Booth, an expert on UFO crash retrievals, agrees that the SADM would have been a logical choice, "Because of the remoteness of the location, a smaller, more tactical nuclear device would probably have been the weapon of choice in this case. Also, the radioactive aftermath would have eliminated any chance of the chemical or biological agent surviving. I am fairly certain that this had a two-fold purpose. Presuming that the soldiers died from chemical or biological agents, it would be the intelligent thing to do to stop the spread of the agent. Also, this would eliminate any and all evidence of that part of the recovery. I am sure that all testing and any retrieval of artifacts was completed first."

The concept of using a nuclear blast to neutralize lethal biological agents has been known to the U.S. Government, and was recently mentioned in a U.S. Department of Energy document called *Radiation-Neutralization of Stored Biological Warfare Agents with Low-Yield Nuclear Warheads*. The report states, "Nuclear explosions produce many effects that can potentially destroy a biological agent. These include blast overpressure, prompt radiation dose, fireball heat, and radiation dose from the delayed gammas and neutrons emitted by the fission debris cloud.... Agent neutralization by the prompt radiation output [is] a potentially attractive kill mechanism of nuclear warheads."

7. WILD RIDE THROUGH TEXAS

At approximately 5:40 p.m. on August 26, the remaining members of the U.S. recovery team made final preparations to depart the Mexican convoy site. Waiting on the desert floor nearby ready to whisk the team away were the three UH-1 Huey helicopters brought in from Fort Bliss. As the team members boarded the choppers, a technician set the mechanical timer on the MK-54 Special Atomic Demolition Munition, verified that a countdown was in progress, and then scrambled to join the others on board the Hueys.

At 5:46 p.m., the three helicopters lifted up off the desert floor and moved away toward the northeast. As the team members increased the distance between themselves and the convoy area, the timer on the MK-54 cycled down to zero, and the device erupted into a ball of flame that burst upward into the clouds. Though it generated a significant explosion, the low-yield device's blast effects were contained within the relatively small area of desert where the Mexican convoy vehicles once stood. All remaining traces of the Coyame incident were obliterated in a fiery furnace equivalent to ten tons of TNT.

A short while later, the Hueys caught up with the Sea Stallion, despite the large aircraft's 26-minute head start. The four helicopters formed a tight formation and re-entered U.S. airspace near Candelaria, Texas. As the team members saw the Rio Grande River recede into the distance behind them, they undoubtedly breathed a sigh of relief to be back over U.S. soil, although their mission was far from over.

With a possibly contaminated extraterrestrial spaceship still dangling at the end of Sea Stallion's cargo cable, the helicopter convoy could not just go where it pleased. The team's immediate priorities were to remain undetected and to prevent any sort of contamination from the alien craft. What remained of the mission called for the greatest amount of stealth and patience on the part of the team.

While in the air over the mountains north of Candelaria, coded

44

orders may have been received on a secure military frequency. The team received instructions to proceed immediately to a previously designated remote location deep within the rugged Davis Mountains.

The helicopters continued on a northeast heading, flying over the southern edge of the Sierra Vieja range, in the area of Capote Peak, which rises to an altitude of 6,212 feet. Clearing the mountains, the helicopters crossed Texas Highway 90 approximately twelve miles southeast of Valentine. This flight path took the aircraft over some of the most sparsely populated terrain in West Texas, thus affording minimal exposure to curious eyes. The helicopters then moved quickly into the nearby Davis Mountains, which are known as the "Texas Alps."

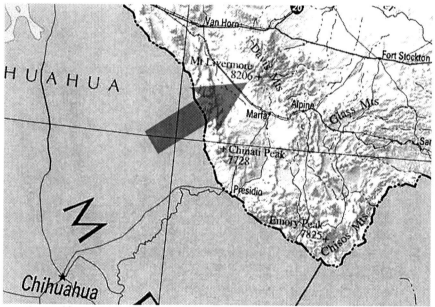

Arrow Shows Approx. Flight Path of U.S. Team After Disk Recovery (Map Courtesy of U.T. Austin Libraries)

The Davis Mountains are the second highest range in Texas. A number of its peaks exceed 7,000 feet, and one peak, Mount Livermore, is the fifth tallest in the state at 8,378 feet. The Davis Mountains extend over a sixty-mile area, forming the shape of a V near the middle of Jeff Davis County. The approximate center of the V is ten miles northwest of the town of Fort Davis. It is because of

45

the remoteness of this area, the high altitude, and the darkness of the nights that the University of Texas maintains a world-class astronomical observatory atop one of the peaks here. With few nearby population centers to generate nighttime light, the observatory's location is ideal. The major road in this area is Texas Highway 118, the state's highest public road, which bisects the Davis Mountains from northwest to southeast, passing through Fort Davis and continuing south to the Big Bend National Park near the Rio Grande River.

It was into the middle of these rugged Davis Mountains that the four helicopters carrying the retrieved UFO flew at approximately 7:00 p.m. on August 26, 1974. The Hueys landed first, in a hidden clearing several miles from the intersection of State Highways 118 and 166. Soldiers, again wearing their CPE protective gear, scrambled out to await the lowering of the UFO from the Sea Stallion's cargo cable. Signaling to the Stallion crew when the disk touched the ground, the soldiers quickly unfastened the helicopter's cable from the straps. Afterward, the Sea Stallion also landed nearby.

Before the arrival of the helicopters, an advance team of soldiers had undoubtedly prepared the landing zone, tightly securing it against any intrusion and possibly bringing in a mobile quarantine unit where the members of the UFO rescue team could wait and rest, while remaining within view of their precious cargo. Although the exact measures taken to ensure the safety of the team members are unknown, they were obviously highly successful, because none of the members of the Coyame recovery effort suffered to any mission-related injury or illness.

The location of the temporary base in the Davis Mountains was chosen for its natural isolation and relative invisibility. The land may have been leased to the federal government, or perhaps government officials made last-minute arrangements with a civilian landowner to use the property temporarily.

In this wild and desolate area, the Coyame recovery team spent several restless hours in the darkness and stillness of the West Texas night, awaiting the next step of their mission. Looking out at the shapes of the pine and oak trees surrounding their encampment, team members may have jumped at every rustling leaf and windblown branch.

Guards in CPE gear patrolled the area. It is possible that most of the team members remained outfitted in their CPE garments all night, fearing that what had killed the Mexican soldiers might still be present. The scene was otherworldly. Nearby, under a drab green tarp was a spacecraft from another world, full of unknown dangers and responsible for the deaths of their Mexican counterparts. And here also were the Coyame team members wearing outfits designed to protect them from nuclear, biological, and chemical contaminants.

They were strangers in a strange land, on a mission that they could never talk about even to their spouses or children. Their careers, and possibly their very lives were at stake.

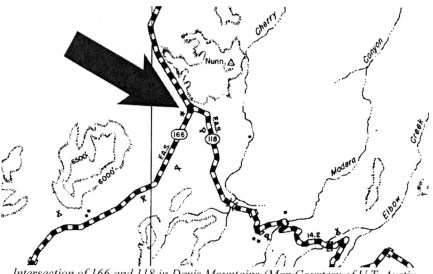

Intersection of 166 and 118 in Davis Mountains (Map Courtesy of U.T. Austin Libraries)

8. HANDING OFF THE PACKAGE

At 2:00 a.m. on Tuesday, August 27, after about seven hours of anxious waiting, conditions were right and the necessary assets were in place for the UFO recovery team to continue its mission. Some 25 miles northwest of the Davis Mountains temporary camp, a small convoy of military trucks moved into position alongside a lonely stretch of country road halfway between the towns of Kent and Van Horn. Heavily armed men in bio-protection suits worked hastily around the trucks, preparing for the arrival of the package they were assigned to escort to its next destination. Among the chores to be completed before the helicopters arrived was the erection of roadblocks in the area to prevent any civilian vehicles from approaching the site.

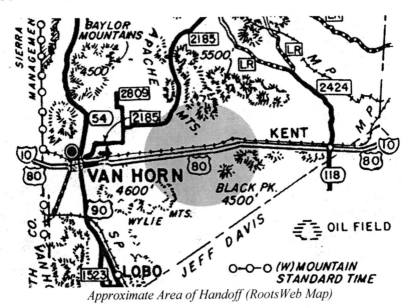

Approximate Area of Handoff (RootsWeb Map)

Back in the Davis Mountains, after the crashed disk was again secured to the cargo cable dangling from the hovering Sea Stallion, the helicopters began the final leg of their journey to a destination only a few minutes away. Under the cover of darkness, illuminated

48

only by a three-quarters moon, the eerie convoy of helicopters with their dangling cargo was over its target in about 15 minutes. A series of signal lights from the ground and encrypted radio communications guided the helicopter crews to the exact location.

Carefully and delicately, the tarp-covered UFO was lowered onto a platform near the largest of the waiting trucks. From there, it was carefully hoisted into the large truck, which was sealed to safely contain any remaining contaminants. With the cargo successfully delivered and positioned inside the transport vehicle, the UFO recovery team breathed a huge sigh of relief.

Before the four helicopters departed from the transfer zone, some of the personnel from the Hueys transferred over to join the truck convoy that would take the disk to its final destination. As the Hueys lifted back up into the air to join the hovering Sea Stallion, the truck drivers started their engines, maneuvered their vehicles onto the narrow road, and sped away into the moonlit night.

As the trucks moved away, the helicopters rose up and proceeded to their original bases, where they were moved to an isolated area for decontamination. The returning team members also underwent decontamination, along with extensive debriefings and a lengthy series of medical examinations, the results of which proved that the team members were completely healthy.

Meanwhile, the convoy of trucks carrying the crashed disk made its way eastward reportedly headed for a destination 1,300 miles from where they picked up their secret cargo. According to the original source of this report, the trucks had been instructed to deliver the flying saucer to a classified location in Atlanta, Georgia.

The anonymous report on the Coyame crash states, "All helicopters then returned to their original bases for decontamination procedures. The convoy continued non-stop, using back roads and smaller highways, and staying away from cities. The destination of the convoy reportedly was Atlanta, Georgia."

UFO crash retrieval expert B.J. Booth believes that Atlanta was chosen because of its world-class biosafety research laboratories comprising the U.S. Government's *Center for Disease Control* (CDC). Booth says, "The military had a very specific reason for taking the object to Georgia, like certain laboratory facilities that fit the testing that needed to be accomplished."

The 1,300-mile trip from near Van Horn, Texas to Atlanta would have been tedious and difficult enough if the convoy had been allowed to use the interstate highways, but it was not. As part of the mission's security protocols, the trucks were to use only back roads and smaller highways. They were also to stay as far away as possible from major population centers. Finally, they were to stop for no reason other than to refuel at certain designated refueling locations along the way.

Military Truck Convoy (U.S. Dept. of Defense Photo)

An interstate route with minimal stops would have taken approximately 21 hours. Given the conditions imposed on the truck convoy, the drive to Atlanta would undoubtedly take closer to 30 hours with many large cities to avoid.

The transportation team certainly regretted not being able to merge right onto Interstate 10 at Kent, Texas. Interstate 10 would have taken them straight through to Mobile, Alabama, where they would have switched over to Interstate 85, which would have delivered them right into downtown Atlanta. They could not take this route because it would meant parading through the middle of several large population centers, including San Antonio, Houston, Baton Rouge, New Orleans, Mobile, and Montgomery.

Instead, the convoy of trucks likely took Texas Highway 118 to the southeast, back toward the Davis Mountains. Then the drivers took a confusing series of twists and turns through West Texas, the Texas Hill Country, and then on to East Texas, all the while avoiding the larger cities. The nightmarish journey then continued through Louisiana, Mississippi, Alabama, and finally Georgia.

Along the way to Atlanta, the convoy bypassed a number of military facilities that could have easily been selected to receive the Coyame materials, if a lethal biological hazard had not been suspected. From the convoy's starting point near Van Horn, Texas, Kirtland Air Force Base in Albuquerque, New Mexico was less than 400 miles. Kirtland has long been suspected of possessing UFO artifacts and of being a site for secret military research on recovered UFOs. Kirtland was also one of the places rumored to have received artifacts from a reported UFO crash near Del Rio, Texas in 1950.

Also bypassed by the convoy was Ellington Air Force Base near Houston, Texas, located about 600 miles away. Some UFO researchers believe tests on recovered extraterrestrial technologies have been conducted over the years at Ellington.

Less than 500 miles from Van Horn is Carlswell Air Force Base in Fort Worth, Texas. A base with a deep history in UFO lore, Carlswell is believed to be the place where some of the wreckage from the 1947 UFO crash near Roswell, New Mexico, was taken.

Nevada's infamous Groom Lake ("Area 51") was only 960 miles away from Van Horn, via mainly desolate desert roads. The most legendary military base in UFO history, Groom Lake is an ultra high security, top-secret base where America's most innovative new aircraft are developed and tested. For decades, UFO researchers have claimed that the military uses Groom Lake to test extraterrestrial technology that has been recovered over the years.

Had the medical research facilities of the CDC not been needed, the convoy could have simply returned the crash debris to where the recovery mission started – Fort Bliss, Texas. From Van Horn, the convoy was a mere 120 miles from the huge base that extends all the way from El Paso into southwestern New Mexico. In this mammoth military compound with its over one million acres of land, the recovered UFO could have been secretly processed, tested, and sent on by plane to other research facilities.

51

Nevertheless, the pre-selected destination for the Coyame materials was altogether different. Carrying perhaps one of the greatest discoveries in human history, the military convoy rumbled slowly toward the laboratories at the Center for Disease Control in Atlanta, Georgia. Once in Georgia, military officials expected that the convoy's unearthly cargo could be safely handled and fully tested for any remaining lethal properties. Perhaps the military believed that if a lethal agent were found, it might be harnessed for use as a weapon.

9. THE CDC AND THE UFO

Originally created in 1942 to fight the spread of malaria and other tropical diseases, the Center for Disease Control in Atlanta, Georgia eventually became America's nerve center for all facets of the war against communicable diseases throughout the world. By 1974, when the Coyame crash retrieval occurred, the CDC had moved far beyond battling the mundane illnesses of humanity's past and was breaking new ground in addressing lethal outbreaks of new and mysterious diseases.

CDC Headquarters in Atlanta, Georgia – Late 1960s (CDC Photo)

Among the CDC's many successes in the middle 1970s were breakthroughs in overcoming Legionnaire's Disease and Toxic Shock Syndrome, as well as being involved in the functional end of endemic smallpox and the wild polio virus. Beginning in 1971, the

CDC also took on the critical responsibility of regulating the use and transport of all potentially harmful biological agents in the United States. As such, it is the agency charged with preventing the release of lethal biological materials either by accident or by deliberate action. This role has expanded after 2001, as Americans grew fearful that terrorists would use biological weapons to maximize casualties in the United States.

By the early 1960s, the CDC had established impressive technologies and procedures for safely and routinely handling lethal biological agents. CDC laboratories fall under one of four possible biosafety classifications, ranging from Biosafety Level 1 (safest) to Biosafety Level 4 (riskiest). In CDC procedures manuals, Biosafety Level 4 is described as follows: "Biosafety Level 4 is required for work with dangerous and exotic agents that pose a high individual risk of aerosol-transmitted laboratory infections and life-threatening disease. Agents with a close or identical antigenic relationship to Biosafety Level 4 agents are handled at this level until sufficient data are obtained either to confirm continued work at this level, or to work with them at a lower level."

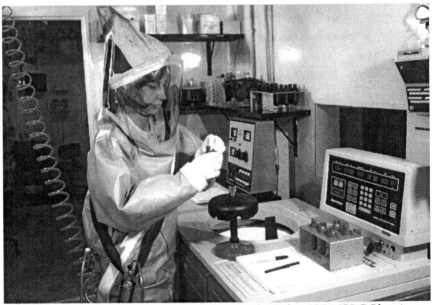

CDC Scientist Working in a BioSafety Level 4 Lab – 1964 (CDC Photo)

"Members of the laboratory staff have specific and thorough training in handling extremely hazardous infectious agents and they understand the primary and secondary containment functions of the standard and special practices, the containment equipment, and the laboratory design characteristics. They are supervised by competent scientists who are trained and experienced in working with these agents. Access to the laboratory is strictly controlled by the laboratory director. The facility is either in a separate building or in a controlled area within a building, which is completely isolated from all other areas of the building.... The Biosafety Level 4 laboratory has special engineering and design features to prevent microorganisms from being disseminated into the environment."

Scientists working within the CDC laboratories are required to put on protective garments that are airtight, thereby, protecting the wearer from exposure to highly infectious pathogenic organisms. Fresh, filtered air is supplied to the interior of the suit via overhead tubing. The positive-pressurization offers some added protection to exposure through a defect in the suit, because if the suit were compromised, air would be forced out of the suit instead of being sucked into the suit.

Without a doubt, if a lethal biological agent was suspected of being present in the Coyame UFO crash debris, the CDC Biosafety Level 4 laboratory in Atlanta, Georgia, was the ideal place for careful research to be conducted on it. As such, it seems reasonable to assume that this lab was the actual destination of the military convoy of trucks that made the long trek from Van Horn, Texas to Atlanta on August 27, 1974.

After about thirty hours on the road, the convoy may have arrived in Atlanta as early as Thursday, August 29. Quietly and discreetly, military and CDC personnel wearing biosafety gear offloaded the convoy's mysterious cargo and took it into CDC BSL 4, as the special laboratory was known.

Keeping the Coyame materials secret while at the CDC was no problem for the military. The CDC is highly secure, with tightly controlled access, carefully compartmentalized operations, and a high level of secrecy, resulting from so much work that is done there for the U.S. Department of Defense. Any records of the Coyame crash materials being examined by CDC personnel would be classified top secret and kept totally out of the public's view. That the military might be considering weaponizing an extraterrestrial biological agent would never be known.

To ensure even more control over the CDCs records, the government's power over what kinds of CDC records are released to the public was greatly increased in 2005 with the introduction of the Sensitive But Unclassified (SBU) policy. Under SBU, the government can refuse to disclose any unclassified information that it would otherwise be required to release if it were labeled as being "sensitive."

CDC Scientist Working in a BioSafety Level 4 Lab – 1978 (CDC Photo)

In August of 1947, the CDC staff, at some point after running a tests designed to find biological contaminants in the Coyame debris, declared the crashed UFO and its contents to be free of any further danger. Perhaps the agent that caused the deaths of the Mexican soldiers was found and removed. Maybe the contaminant had been expended before the debris arrived in Atlanta. Or perhaps there never had been a biological contamination at all.

UFO researcher B.J. Booth, after reading through the evidence in the Coyame crash retrieval, feels that the Mexican soldiers probably died from exposure to toxic chemicals that were venting from the crashed vehicle. After the chemicals were expended into the atmosphere, they may have no longer been concentrated enough to cause any further problems. Booth thinks that a biological contamination probably did not happen, although the U.S. military could not absolutely rule it out until after CDC scientists in Atlanta fully tested the recovered materials.

When the examination in Atlanta was concluded, the military again took possession of the Coyame crashed disk and moved it to a secure military location. The report on the Coyame incident states, "Here the hard evidence thins out. One unconfirmed report says the disk was eventually transferred to Wright-Patterson Air Force Base. Another says that the disk was either transferred after that to another unnamed base, or was taken directly to this unknown base from Atlanta." Thus, this is where the trail of the Coyame crash artifacts runs absolutely cold.

10. The Physical Evidence

The descriptions of the crashed disk recovered near Coyame are based on the recollections of two persons who were reportedly witnesses to the events of August 1974. The exact role that these eyewitnesses played in the drama is not known; however, the account based on their testimony is intriguing and captivating.

They describe the disk as being sixteen feet, five inches in diameter, and equally convex on both upper and lower surfaces. There was an outer "rim" around the central circumference of the disk. This type of UFO shape has been called a "Saturn" disk or "double dome."

Drawing of 1958 Saturn Disk UFO Sighting (NICAP)

The height of the object was slightly less than five feet. They saw no visible portholes, doors, or markings. In addition, no lights of any kind were apparent. There was also no obvious mechanism for propulsion. The external surface of the disk was like silvery polished steel.

The outer rim of the disk showed damage in two places. One damage point was an irregular hole about 12 inches in diameter with material from the metallic surface of the disk "indented" around the jagged hole. None of the witnesses reported seeing anything inside this hole. This puncture damage was believed by the witnesses to have resulted from the mid-air collision between the flying disk and the small civilian aircraft.

The other damage point was a two-foot-wide "dent." The witnesses believed the dent to have been caused by the disk's fall to earth after its collision with the plane.

The weight of the object was about 1,500 pounds, according to eyewitness estimates based on the lifting of the disk by the Sea Stallion helicopter and on the transferring of the disk from the helicopter to the truck for its ground transport.

Regarding the possible recovery of bodies from the crash site, witnesses mention nothing about any UFO occupants seen in or around the crashed disk. However, UFO researcher Robert Dean of Phoenix, Arizona, has in his possession a photograph of a small "grey" alien that Dean thinks may have been recovered in the Coyame crash.

Photograph Given to Robert Dean (Used By Permission)

In the mid-1990s, Dean was attending a UFO conference in Mexico City when a Mexican policeman approached him with a fascinating revelation. Taking out a small black and white photograph, the officer explained that the picture showed an alien being that had been captured by the Mexican Federal police at the site of an unspecified UFO crash.

59

The officer stated that he knew the photo to be legitimate and that the alien in the picture was authentic. Dean was very impressed by the police officer's sincere and serious demeanor. "The policeman ... did not specify anything about the incident except that the grey was uninjured and in fairly good health," Dean said.

"Being as always cautious and somewhat dubious of such situations, I accepted the picture and thanked him for his efforts," Dean recalls. Dean views this as "a very likely authentic photograph of a small grey."

If not recovered in the Coyame crash, this grey might be the occupant of the UFO that crashed near Mexico City in December of 1949, which is discussed in a later chapter. The Mexico City alien was described as being about two-feet tall with a "very large head and small body." This description is also very close to that of the badly burned occupant of a 1948 UFO crash reported near Laredo, Texas.

Regarding the crashed saucer retrieved from Coyame, sometimes UFO crash stories trace the recovered artifacts to a specific location and offer descriptions of them as given by later witnesses. Unfortunately, that is not the case for the Coyame UFO. As the truck convoy disappeared into the night, the remnants of the crashed UFO forever vanished from the published record. The hasty departure left some significant and troubling unanswered questions.

For example, who were the occupants of the small plane bound from El Paso to Mexico City, and what happened to their remains? UFO researchers have searched FAA files for any record pertaining to such a flight on the night of August 25, 1974, but have found nothing. Some have speculated that no records ever existed because the plane was of Mexican registration, while others believe that the government confiscated the records.

Also unknown is the exact cause of death for the Mexican recovery team. No documentation exists to suggest that any of the U.S. team members suffered any ill effects from their involvement in the UFO recovery, despite many hours of being in close proximity to the crashed disk.

Another troubling question is why the U.S. team made no effort to recover one or more of the bodies of the Mexican soldiers for further study. This might suggest that the team did not take with them the necessary equipment to transport a body with a suspected lethal contaminant. Or, perhaps determining the cause of the Mexicans' deaths was either not a priority or not necessary at all. Maybe the U.S. intelligence community was already familiar with the causal agent.

Also puzzling is the lack of evidence from within Mexico. There is certainly a Mexican paper trail somewhere. The airplane that crashed was from Mexico. The persons killed in the plane crash were probably Mexican citizens. The 12 to 24 Mexican soldiers who participated in the initial recovery effort certainly left family and friends behind who would have inquired into their demise. Someone in the area of the crash site must have heard and possibly seen something.

In addition, the early radio communications between the Mexican recovery team and their base must be documented somewhere. The mention of a second crash site and initial description of the crashed disk was certainly heard by Mexican military personnel back in Chihuahua. After all, someone was sufficiently concerned to declare an immediate radio silence.

Mexican UFO journalist, Jaime Maussan, who has studied the Coyame crash, has said that fear has kept many Mexicans from disclosing what they know about the incident. In 2005, Maussan told *The History Channel*, "I was recently in Chihuahua, and I asked about this case, and there is a rumor that there are photographs around this case that I haven't seen. I was promised that I was going to receive these photographs, but people here, they are still afraid. It seems that they have kept these photographs for a long, long time."

Fear is certainly a great motivator, and it has been used successfully in the past to keep UFO evidence hidden away for decades. Some witnesses fear the UFO occupants, others fear the government authorities, and some just have a generalized fear that if they speak up, something bad will happen to them.

As of the writing of this book, precious little additional information has been uncovered regarding what might be one of the most incredible events in the history of mankind. The Coyame incident certainly rivals the story of alleged UFO crash near Roswell, New Mexico in 1947.

As for the evidence that we do have about the Coyame crash, where exactly did it come from? The details included in this book about this event all come from an amazing document that was first disclosed to the public in the early 1990s. The story of the original disclosure of this incredible story is recounted in our next chapter.

11. THE MYSTERIOUS DENEB REPORT

Rumors of a UFO crash near Coyame persisted for nearly 20 years before the story finally came out, in a document called *Research Findings on the Chihuahua Disk Crash*, composed in 1992 by members of an anonymous group calling itself the "Deneb team." The report may have first been posted on an online bulletin board service (BBS), a dial-up information sharing service that was prevalent before Internet access became commonplace in America. The report, authored by someone identified only as *JS*, was addressed to "All Deneb Team Members."

In the summer of 1993, Elaine Douglass, who at that time was an officer for the Washington, D.C. UFO group *Operation Right to Know*, received a copy of the *Research Findings on Chihuahua Disk Crash*. Douglass, who holds a Master's degree in military policy from M.I.T., opened her mailbox one day and found the mysterious document with no evidence of who sent it, other than a postmark from Santa Ana, California. Douglass thus became one of the very first civilian UFO researchers to see the document. In a statement written exclusively for this book, Douglass shares her insights into the Coyame incident.

Elaine Douglass, 1993 Photo

Douglass believes that the "Chihuahua Disk Crash" report was created by employees within the government's intelligence community who gathered scraps of UFO-related information over many years. Although these individuals likely did not have sufficient security clearance to be "officially" in the know, they managed to collect important data, which eventually fit together perfectly, like pieces of a jigsaw puzzle. Despite not having access to any physical evidence from the Coyame UFO crash, these government employees, who referred to themselves as "Deneb team," managed to connect the dots and come up with the amazing scenario described in the *Research Findings on Chihuahua Disk Crash*. They then shared their findings within a small network of trusted acquaintances possibly using an electronic bulletin board system.

Douglass speculates that groups like the "Deneb team" exist within the government and that they collect and share information among their members regarding incidents such as the recovery of extraterrestrial artifacts. She feels certain that a number of people who have served in government are fully aware of the reality of UFOs. Further, there are individuals within government who seem determined to amass information about this topic, although their exact motives for doing so are not clear. One is left to wonder what their intent is, as very little of this information ever seems to come out into the public view.

Douglass considers it critical to understand that government employees who stumble upon UFO secrets are, like all of us, curious human beings. Although they feel obligated to keep secret what they have learned, they are no less eager to learn more of the matter than we would be. From their vantage point, they are better able than we to recognize traces of governmental cover-ups, and occasionally, they may actually stumble across hard facts of a documented alien contact. Undoubtedly, these government employees are, like we, consumed by curiosity and transfixed by the importance of the topic of extraterrestrial visitations to Earth. However, unlike civilians, they cannot openly speak or write about what they know. Fear and implied threats keep them silent. So what can they do if they desire to reveal what they know? According to Douglass, the answer to this question may lie in the Deneb team's report.

Douglass characterizes the Deneb team as a "quiet little informal study group" composed of like-minded government employees seeking to uncover the truth about a specific UFO incident. She feels these types of informal study groups may be a typical method used by groups of trusted acquaintances to discuss and share what they have learned about UFOs. These groups, operating with great secrecy and anonymity, also involve themselves in discretely collecting information about UFO events such as the Coyame crash retrieval.

Douglass thinks that the author of the "Chuhuahua Disk Crash" document, identified as *JS*, somehow obtained access to written government reports regarding the Coyame crash. JS makes a number of references throughout the document to written sources, such as in stating that "no mention is made of the occupants of the civilian aircraft." Apparently, JS is summarizing the content of one or more documents in which the events of the Chihuahua crash are described.

Additionally, JS seems to refer to several verbal conversations that have taken place regarding the Coyame event. He refers to several "unconfirmed" reports. This suggests that JS has had a number of conversations with others on the Deneb team, while diligently working to piece together a number of disjointed bits of information they have gathered.

More importantly, JS refers to at least one "eyewitness." Douglass thinks this witness was a government employee or soldier stationed at the Fort Bliss Army Base in 1974. Although the eyewitness was probably not involved in the Coyame recovery operation, apparently he or she watched from afar as the recovery team was assembled and knew some important specifics about the mission. Douglass speculates that the witness may have been a woman, perhaps a civilian employee of the base, because while her observations are detailed and factual, she does not seem to be intimately familiar with the exact models of the aircraft used in the operation. Most male base employees would probably have known the exact type of each aircraft.

The document itself is a fairly straightforward recitation of facts that have been collected by JS and others. There is nothing in the document that sheds light as to what type of position or rank the author may have held at the time of the events described. Again, the document appears to result from efforts by individuals within the government to collect and share bits of classified information about UFOs that they have pieced together from various sources. The author of the document does not seem overly concerned about the possible consequences of being found out by his or her superiors; however, there is clearly an effort to remain anonymous.

An interesting side note is the designation FILE UFO3263, which appears at the top of the original Chihuahua Disk Crash report. Douglass believes this indicates that the Coyame crash information is only one of a larger body of carefully cataloged UFO documents. This catalog is obviously maintained by the same clandestine UFO research group consisting of current and former U.S. government employees. One might also infer from the use of the term UFO that this term is actually used in "official" government classified documents, which is something that the U.S. security agencies have steadfastly denied.

Toward what end is this UFO material being assembled and catalogued? Although the information is shared among the members of internal, closed groups, these same members do not seem particularly interested in disclosing what they know to the general public. Douglass believes that this stems from the fact that although they view themselves as deserving to know classified UFO secrets, they do not feel that the general public should know. Due to their positions, they are unable or unwilling to reveal what they know, nor do they want their information indiscriminately trumpeted to the masses by civilian UFO researchers. Thus, the information remains locked away in these quiet little study groups.

Douglass does not believe that *Research Findings on Chihuahua Disk Crash* was leaked by anyone associated with the Deneb team, but rather that a portion of it was stolen from the group and later mailed to civilian UFO investigators, including herself.

According to Douglass, it is also not entirely outside the realm of possibility that the Deneb team was not an informal, unofficial study group but rather an official one, sanctioned by some branch or unit of the U.S. government to uncover facts about the Coyame UFO crash. It is possible that the Deneb team was assembled and tasked by a high government official with a staff, a budget, and the authority to conduct an inquiry into a classified government operation.

Historically, it appears that UFO evidence is such a tightly held secret that it has even been kept from high elected officials, including possibly the President of the United States. The truth about UFOs is genuinely held to a strict "need to know" doctrine. Therefore, a high government official, feeling out of the loop and at a serious disadvantage on this issue, might desire to conduct an inquiry into specific events such as the Coyame event in an effort to become better educated on the matter.

Let's suppose that a government official, elected or appointed, desires to uncover UFO evidence that he or she suspects exists. His motivation might be a deep personal interest in the extraterrestrial matter; or, perhaps knowledge of extraterrestrials is seen as a means of advancing his career in government. If a high official amasses a cabinet-full of data on UFO crash retrievals, this information can surely be useful to secure funding, to gain more powerful positions, to sit on influential committees, and so on.

Whatever its origin, the Deneb report was clearly not intended for release to the general public. It was meant to be circulated only within the members of the Deneb team. However, it was at some point stolen from the Deneb team, re-typed, and then circulated outside the team. Eventually, someone anonymously mailed out copies of the report to several UFO researchers.

After finishing her analysis of the Deneb report, Elaine Douglass adds this fascinating footnote, "While I was MUFON state director for Washington D.C., and well before I received the Deneb team document in the mail, I was contacted by an individual recently discharged from the military who told me something of interest indirectly related to the Mexican disk crash."

"The individual told me that while he was in the military, he served with a unit whose function was to go inside foreign countries, perform some task and get out quickly without the government of the foreign country knowing the unit had been there."

Douglass says that she met with her informant, a man in his late thirties, in a Washington D.C. coffee shop, "He showed me his military records, which were in plastic sleeves in a 3-ring binder. He said that the unit he served with was stationed in the United States and was not unique. That is, that there are several such teams in readiness at all times."

Douglass remembers her informant saying that the rapid-deploy missions he had been involved in were always extremely high stress, and that it took the team members a long time after completion of their object to "unwind" and return to normalcy. According to the source, soldiers returning from these stealth missions were tense to the point of irrationality for a long period afterward. Anyone who irritated one of these men was in serious danger of being "punched out" by them.

According to Douglass, the informant did not describe in great detail any specific missions his rapid-deploy teams had performed. Also, he did not state that he himself had been involved in any UFO crash recoveries. However, he did indicate that recovering crashed UFO artifacts would have been well within the scope of the types of missions these groups undertook and had in fact undertaken in the past. "I recall him saying that he and his fellow servicemen used to stay up late at night talking about UFOs and extraterrestrials and wondering what was their ultimate significance," Douglass explains.

Douglass believes that the rapid-deploy stealth team described in the *Research Findings on Chihuahua Disk Crash* document is exactly the type of unit that her anonymous ex-military informant was talking about. The quick incursion into Mexico, the destruction of the evidence, the recovery of the disk, and the clandestine truck convoy from Texas to Atlanta via less-traveled roads were the very kinds of activities described to Douglass by the man she met in Washington D.C.

"The one thing my informant told me I will never forget—he said his team had standing orders not to return any bodies. On the face of it this would have to include human or extraterrestrial bodies." Douglass feels this could indicate that the U.S. government already has already made a large number of UFO body recoveries and that the recovery of bodies is no longer a priority.

The complete Deneb report, as it first appeared in the early 1990s, is found in Appendix A of this book. Appendix E contains the complete, original statement given to us by Elaine Douglass in 2006, regarding the Coyame UFO crash.

After receiving her copy of the *Chihuahua Disk Crash* report,

Douglass immediately passed along a copy of it to Leonard H. Stringfield, a pioneer UFO crash retrieval researcher. Stringfield included the account in his final report on UFO crash retrievals, published in February 1994 and titled *UFO Crash/Retrievals: Search for Proof in a Hall of Mirrors (Status Report IV)*. In publishing the account, Stringfield told his readers that he had previously avoided UFO stories from anonymous sources, but that "there seems to be a legitimacy to the 1974 Chihuahua crash report." Stringfield described the account as "authoritatively written, using correct military terminology and, of note and unlike a hoax, draws a line between so-called 'hard evidence' and that which is speculative."

Stringfield added, "... I heard of the Chihuahua case before, either in the late 1970s or early 1980s. The only detail I vaguely recall is that a U.S. military team had covertly crossed into Mexico to retrieve the object."

In addition to the copy sent to Elaine Douglass, the report was also mailed anonymously to several other UFO researchers in the U.S. and Britain from 1993 to 1996. In his 2005 book *Majic Eyes Only: Earth's Encounters With Extraterrestrial Technology*, UFO researcher Ryan S. Wood states, "The report appears to have been written by a source or sources with intimate knowledge of the incident at issue who desired the release of the evidence to interested parties."

UFO researcher B.J. Booth agrees, "I am sure the informant was not one of a lower rank, or clerical person. There is not any way that one 'not in the loop' could be privy to the type of information that was covered in the Chihuahua account. In my opinion, and I cannot prove this, I would say that the informant would have been an active military person of high regard who was involved heavily in the actual seizure and relocation of the crash debris - probably military intelligence."

As there were a number of other UFO reports posted on various bulletin board systems by a "JS" addressed to "All Deneb Team Members," this appears to have been a clandestine group of UFO researchers, operating possibly within the U.S. government, who were active in the 1980s and early 1990s.

The most striking aspect of the Deneb report is that it sounds entirely plausible. It stands up to careful scrutiny, even after closely correlating all events to a timeline, plotting on maps all movements described, and carefully checking other facts mentioned therein for historical and logistical accuracy. The information most certainly came from a person or persons who either actually witnessed the events or read original source documents about those events.

"The Coyame case is extremely intriguing, and I have no reason at this time to doubt it," B.J. Booth says. "This could be one of the very best UFO crash and recovery cases, if more witness corroboration, and documentation could be made available."

The Deneb report is said to have originated with two eyewitnesses, some illegally copied documents, and one partially destroyed document. The illegal copying was done in 1978, and the person who copied the documents subsequently died. The copied documents apparently contained the written accounts of two persons who witnessed some or all of the events.

It is also noteworthy that Leonard Stringfield recalled first having heard of a Chihuahua, Mexico UFO crash "either in the late 1970s or early 1980s." That means Stringfield heard the story very shortly after the original documents were leaked, sometime after 1978.

Interestingly, the release of the Deneb report came 18 years after the actual events. That's about the number of years it would take for individuals who were in their forties in 1974 to reach retirement age. If this report did indeed originate with persons who experienced the events firsthand, it makes sense that they waited until their retirement from military service to disclose.

12. COYAME'S DARK SECRET

At first glance, the remote Mexican desert town of Coyame seems the most unlikely of places for something of this magnitude to happen. The sleepy hamlet of about 2,000 residents serves primarily as a pit stop for motorists navigating the lonely 139-mile stretch of Mexican Federal Highway 16 between the busy border town of Ojinaga and the state capital of Chihuahua City. Although located a mere 50 miles from the Texas border, Coyame, with its mostly unpaved roads and minimal infrastructure, seems light years removed from the nearby towns on the U.S. side of the border, such as Presidio and Marfa.

Coyame Town Hall (2006 by Ruben Uriarte)

To travelers on Highway 16, Coyame springs up suddenly amidst the hills and mountains of this rugged part of Mexico's vast Chihuahuan desert. Cruising through town, drivers see a number of plain, unremarkable buildings, including the town hall, a tiny library, two churches, a school, a restaurant, a gas station, and a few residences. A grassy, tree-lined town square, or *plaza*, serves as a daily gathering place for local residents.

Were it not for what is rumored to have happened near here in 1974, it is doubtful that Coyame would be circled as a destination on the maps of a great many visitors to this desolate area. Regardless, the town does bring in *some* tourist dollars due to its proximity to two highly regarded natural attractions. On a dirt road just south of town, the Coyame Caverns feature fifteen rooms full of interesting formations, said to be among the best in northern Mexico. Twenty miles to the north of the caverns is the spectacular Peguis Canyon overlook above the Conchos River. From the overlook, visitors peer two thousand feet down to the bottom of the canyon, which extends as far to the horizon as the eye can see.

Coyame Caverns (2006 by Ruben Uriarte)

In Coyame, one feels the stillness of time and is often alone with his thoughts as each quiet day unfolds without the hustle and rush of city life. Sitting on a concrete bench in the town square, one has time to reflect on life, as gentle breezes stir the warm desert air. Life is reduced to simple terms here, as local residents struggle to eke out a living from the rocky desert by farming, ranching, or mining. The raising of cattle, goats, chickens, horses, and ostriches generates most of the income here, as does the growing of walnuts, apricots, date palms, figs, watermelons, and melons. Found in nearby hills and mountains are deposits of silver, sodium chloride, lead, copper, manganese, fluorita, onyx, baryta, and uranium.

Although some 2,000 souls live within the boundaries of the town itself, many others live and work in the numerous ranches that dot the mountainous landscape in all directions around Coyame. Doing research on reported UFO events is slow, tedious, and often unproductive among these small, close-knit ranching communities in the rugged and isolated mountains of this region. Since the early 1990s, when the report of a 1974 UFO crash in the mountains near Coyame first surfaced, interviews with the locals have yielded precious few details about this unprecedented event. However, the little information that has surfaced in this area remains extremely interesting.

The Desert Just North of Coyame (2007 by Ruben Uriarte)

Prior to investigations launched by authors of this book, possibly the only UFO researcher to have spent time talking to residents of the ranches around Coyame is Gilberto E. Rivera Altamirano, director of GIFAE (Group for the Investigation of Aerial Phenomena) in Chihuahua City. Although it continues to be a slow and difficult process for him, Rivera is convinced that he will eventually find persons with information about the 1974 UFO crash retrieval. "We located a rancher, Carlos Valenzuela, whose property is adjacent to where a U.S. Pershing missile crashed near *El Cuervo* in 1967," Rivera said. "We think that most of what he remembers is related to the Pershing missile crash rather than a UFO event, but

Mr. Valenzuela has agreed to help us find other people in the area who may have specific information about the 1974 incident."

Rivera has adopted a strategy of trying to find persons who were living in the area in 1974. He has focused his search in the area around three ranches located north of Coyame: *Potrero del Llano*, *Las Palmitas*, and *El Cuervo*. It is in the area around the ranch known as *El Llano* that Chihuahua attorney Jorge A. González Almeida believes the 1974 UFO crash occurred. *El Llano*, which in English means "the plain," is a flat area between mountain ranges, located approximately 40 miles north of Coyame.

Unfortunately, so many years after the fact, the memories many longtime Coyame-area residents have become indistinct. "Interestingly, we recently ran across information about the crash in 1985 of a small aircraft being used by drug traffickers," Rivera added. "That crash took place about 20 miles north of Coyame." According to Rivera, sometimes the memories of these similar events get mixed together in the minds the old-time residents of these remote ranches. An object is seen streaking across the sky before slamming into the ground, military officials cordon off the crash site, and the locals are left to speculate as to the exact details of the incident.

Javier Baeza Nieto, a longtime Coyame rancher and president of the local cattlemen's association, is also very interested in finding out more about the 1974 crash near his town. Interviewed by the authors in his small office in Coyame in October of 2006, Baeza recalls that while attending a gathering of local residents some years ago, he heard a former police officer, Eduardo Cervantes, say that he had visited the crash site of a small airplane north of Coyame in the mid to late 1970s. "The wreckage was still smoldering in the morning when he went out there. Apparently the crash had happened sometime during the night. Eduardo did not know what caused the crash or whether a UFO was involved. He just witnessed the still-burning wreckage and then had to leave." Baeza added, "I realize this information is secondhand, and I personally didn't even live in this area back then," Baeza said. "I am telling you only exactly what I heard from Eduardo, because to add anything else would be a lie." The former policeman's story of the flaming plane wreckage stands out in Baeza's mind, and he recalls that the eyewitness said it occurred in the vicinity of *Santo Niño* or *El Saucito*. "I don't know if it's related to the UFO crash of 1974," Baeza admits.

Baeza also remembers another local resident, Roberto Arroyo, who told him of an unusual event that occurred at *Rancho Las Paredes*, also near Coyame, involving the apparent crash landing of an unidentified aircraft. Arroyo told Baeza that armed men in military-style uniforms quickly swarmed the crash site; however, the locals were not sure if the soldiers were Mexicans or Americans. The military men scoured the area, looking for pieces of the crash debris.

"Another local resident, Rafa Sanchez, also told me about a similar event," Baeza said. "He said that something fell to the earth and that soldiers came looking for it."

Deep in Thought With Eyes Closed, Baeza Recalls a UFO Encounter (2006 by Ruben Uriarte)

"These are all things we speculate about," Baeza said. "We have no direct evidence. Scientific people will always say it is not true and that we imagined it." Still, he notes, most of Coyame's residents have "an eerie story or two" to tell about things they have seen in the desert sky late at night.

Baeza adds that a large obstacle to finding out more about the 1974 event is that many of the people who lived in the Coyame area at the time have since moved to Ojinaga or other cities or ranches in Mexico. Other former residents, he said, have immigrated to the United States.

One person who remains convinced that the truth about 1974 will eventually be discovered somewhere in the Coyame area is Baeza's friend, Coyame ranch owner Jorge A. González Almeida. Although he resides in Chihuahua City, González spends virtually every weekend on his beloved *El Murcielago* ranch, just north of Coyame. González says he has heard stories from residents of neighboring ranches about a mysterious object that came out of the sky and impacted the desert floor near *El Llano* ranch in around 1974.

Jorge Gonzalez Almeida (2007 by Ruben Uriarte)

González also recalls one of his uncles telling him that the *El Llano* object landed in the field or cattle pasture and that several people had seen circular markings or imprints on the ground of something having landed. According to González, there has been no plant growth in the area where the markings were observed.

The 1974 event is not the only story of strange objects landing

76

amidst the isolated ranchlands north of Coyame, González said. "A number of local people have reported seeing strange flying objects landing in remote areas of their ranches. Others have seen markings on the desert soil suggesting that something had landed there. I myself have seen these kinds of markings."

An example of these many other strange tales comes from Baeza, who recalls something very unusual that happened to him on March 21, 2003. "It had rained a lot out at Jorge González' ranch, and it took us a long time to navigate the muddy roads," Baeza remembers.

"At about two o'clock in the morning, we finally cleared the arroyo near *Cerros Colorados* and headed across the mesa back out toward the highway when suddenly we saw hovering above the horizon before us seven brightly lit objects. One of the objects would shoot away from the others in the direction of the Peguis Canyon and then would come back to rejoin the others."

Baeza describes the objects as roughly cigar-shaped and alternating in color from a light blue to a deeply intense green. Although they hovered generally in a straight line along the horizon, each of the objects exhibited independent motion and seemed in a constant state of movement and fluctuation. Some of the objects would break out of the formation, speed away, and then return. "I would describe their movement as almost playful," Baeza said. "They seemed to play with each other, darting in and out of the line formation."

Baeza remembers hearing no sound from the objects. Although he finds it difficult to estimate the distance of the objects from their vantage point, he says that they seemed fairly close by and at a low altitude.

"We saw this activity not just for a minute or two. We watched the strange shapes in the sky for about fifteen minutes." Baeza remembers turning to González as they viewed the objects and telling him, "You know that if we tell anyone what we're seeing, they are going to think we were on marijuana or crazy or something."

The scene that had unfolded before the two men amazed González, but unfortunately, he was not carrying a camera with him. "Now I always carry a camera with me when I'm out at the ranch,"

González says. "Sooner or later, I will see something like this again and take pictures."

Baeza had an equally disconcerting encounter in the same general area where he and his brother were working one day at about 6 p.m. Following along in his pickup truck as his brother rode on horseback, Baeza suddenly waved and shouted to his brother, who was some distance away, telling him to look up toward a nearby mountain range. What Baeza saw was a strange square object had appeared without warning in the evening sky. Baeza remembers yelling, "Look up there to the left. There is a very bright reflection – there against the mountain."

Mountains Surrounding Coyame (2006 by Ruben Uriarte)

Baeza describes the object as a rotating square that seemed to "come out" of the mountain. As the square rotated in a certain manner, an intense white light shone in all directions, almost like a mirror reflecting light, but much brighter. Then, as suddenly as it appeared, the strange object faded away.

Regarding the Coyame UFO crash itself, Baeza and other local residents do not have much information. A recent article from a magazine published by Mexico City UFO investigator Jaime Maussan notes, "Curiously, this Mexican UFO incident seems to be much better known in foreign countries and in foreign media sources than it is in Mexico."

In July 2005, Maussan sent a team of investigators to Coyame, and the members of the group met with several Coyame residents who lived in the area in 1974. Maussan's team later reported, "We perceived that that there was a general unwillingness to provide us with any concrete information." In fact, only two individuals came forward with stories that seemed related to the 1974 event.

Cipriano Orozco, one of the townspeople, stated, "Yes, several people commented about this incident ... that a UFO had crashed with a small plane, but that the wreckage had been quickly recovered and removed. Not much else was known. What I did see was the movement of troops through this area. But in reality, this whole thing was tightly sealed with few leaks. However, I did hear that it happened."

Emma Ortega, another local resident, gave an account of having seen the smouldering wreckage of a crashed aircraft, a story very similar to what former policeman Eduardo Sanchez once told Baerga. Ortega said, "We knew that it crashed, and we went to go see it. We saw parts of the aircraft scattered on the ground, and it was still on fire. We were not allowed to get up close, and by the time we went to see it, other things had already been removed from there. We never saw what else might have been there."

Maussan's investigative team then continued its search by carefully examining the town's public records archives, with the cooperation of the local authorities. "We found census reports, marriage licenses, birth certificates, and death certificates from as far back as 120 years ago, but we found nothing about the events of 1974."

While the team was in town looking for more information, the members got the impression that an unseen lid clamped down tightly on the truth. "Suddenly, Coyame became like a ghost town. The streets emptied. The businesses closed. Not a single vehicle was seen moving. Suddenly, nobody knew anything. Nobody remembered a thing ... or maybe *nobody wanted to talk about it.*"

Maussan's team next visited some of the desert areas around Coyame, looking for what might have been the crash site. They found one area that they speculated might have been the place, although how they selected it is unknown.

After failing to turn up much information in Coyame, the team moved its investigation to Chihuahua City, where they scoured local newspapers from 1974 were for possible leads. They found only one possibly pertinent item, an article from the October 27, 1974 edition of the *Chihuahua Herald* regarding the death of one Mexican soldier and injuries sustained by others in a "military transport" accident. Very few details about the accident are given in the article. Could this accident have been somehow related to the UFO incident two months earlier? Were the deaths of the Mexican soldiers explained away by a series of cover stories about various military accidents?

Maussan's team concluded by saying, "Will we someday learn the truth about what happened on that day in 1974? The answer is still up in the air."

13. THE SEARCH FOR WITNESSES

The area around Coyame has long been known for eerie and frightening events. Jorge A. González Almeida, the Chihuahua attorney, told the authors, "I personally have witnessed numerous unexplained phenomena at my ranches." González, who operates hunting tours of his properties under the name *CoyameHunting.com*, adds, "The desert sky is extremely clear, and you see things out here that are beyond the normal. Sitting here, gazing into the sky, whether at night or in the daytime, you see often strange things."

Mountains Surrounding Coyame (Courtesy of Jorge González)

"Frequently seen over the ranch are mysterious lights in the sky, which, because of the manner in which they move, are obviously not man-made aircraft," González said, "Most recently, in March of 2005, I and two other persons observed for nearly three hours a group of three of these strange lights. The lights we saw that evening pulsated as they moved in a triangle formation at tremendous speed across the night sky before suddenly coming to a dead stop. During the sighting, an intense whirlwind destroyed the road that leads to the ranch."

González tells an equally bizarre tale about an experience that one of his uncles had in the very same area in 2003. "It was in the darkness of the morning, before dawn broke, that my uncle saw an amazing thing," González recounts. "Suddenly, an intensely-bright white light shone down upon the land, illuminating a nearby mountain range for kilometers in each direction." González says that his uncle watched in stunned silence as the light bathed the surrounding mountains for several seconds before the whole region was instantly returned to darkness.

"Because the area is rich in uranium deposits, my uncle thought that perhaps some kind of chemical reaction had taken place, causing the entire mountain range to become illuminated," González explains, but he admits that he is not satisfied by that explanation.

Like other Coyame residents, González has heard rumors over the years that a UFO-related event occurred near their city in the 1970s. However, few specifics about the crash were known until after the Deneb report was made public in the middle 1990s. Some critics of the Coyame crash have questioned why no person living in Coyame in 1974 has come forward to corroborate the story. A study of the geography of the area and circumstances of this event may help explain this mystery.

Since the crash occurred in the desert perhaps as much as 60 miles from town, it is unlikely that Coyame's residents knew exactly what had happened. The townspeople may have heard or felt distant explosions, but it is unlikely they experienced much else. On the morning after the crash, they may have heard the spotter planes flying overhead, but it is doubtful that they saw the Mexican military convoy that moved into the area later, as the soldiers probably bypassed Coyame and used the system of dirt roads that crisscrosses the desert to reach the two crash sites. Thus, it is almost certain that residents of the town of Coyame had very little access to information about this extraordinary event.

The Mexican soldiers, as they conducted their operations to recover the crashed disk, would have taken other measures to prevent civilians from approaching the crash site. Once the military arrived on the scene at approximately 8 a.m. on August 26, it would have been difficult for any of the townspeople to gain access to any information. Within a couple of hours of their arrival, the soldiers had secured the wreckage of the disk and the small airplane, and their convoy had begun moving across the desert toward either Ojinaga or Chihuahua. By around 11 a.m. on the 26th, there would have been very little left to see at the original crash sites.

It is possible that someone in Coyame saw the explosion in the sky resulting from the two aircraft colliding. It seems unlikely, though, that these eyewitnesses would have gone out wandering around in the dark, dangerous desert at night looking for an impact crater. It is more likely that, like the Mexican military, they would have waited until daybreak to go in search of whatever crashed. However, by early the next morning, Mexican soldiers were in control of the entire area where the crashes occurred.

Giovanna Michelle Rogers Ramirez contacted the authors of this book early in 2006 with a story about a 1974 UFO sighting in Coyame. Now residing in Orange County, California, Ramirez remembers being told about the UFO by her mother, who was born and raised in Coyame. "The year was 1974, she was eleven years old, it was evening time, and my mom and a group of friends were sitting outside of my grandparents' house which is located right in front of a little park called *La Plaza,*" Ramirez recalls.

"All of a sudden, my mom said, they had seen a 'big round object with lights surrounding it,' which was hovering and staying in one position in the northern sky [toward Texas]." Ramirez says that her grandfather thought it was some kind of American military "project," but her mother disagreed and thought it was something not of the earth. Years later, when Ramirez's mom went to study in Mexico City, she heard many stories about UFO activity in Coyame and was convinced that she herself had seen a flying saucer back in 1974.

A significant point about Ramirez's story is that Coyame residents tended to blame unexplained aerial events on American military hardware and activities. Ramirez's family was surely familiar with a number of U.S. test missile crashes in northern Mexico, dating back to the late 1940s. These missile failures, which will be more fully discussed in a later chapter of this book, continued well into the 1960s and early 1970s.

Just seven years prior to the Coyame event, on September 12, 1967, a U.S. Pershing medium-range ballistic missile, designed to carry a nuclear payload, spun out of control and crashed in Chihuahua state near the Texas-Mexico border. The crash coincidentally occurred in virtually the same area as the reported UFO crash of 1974. Crash debris was found in *El Cuervo*, located approximately 100 miles, as the crow flies, from Coyame. The 1967 crash was certainly still fresh in the minds of area residents.

The 10,000-pound Pershing test missile, fired from Utah and targeted for southern New Mexico, exploded on Mexican soil, sparking a minor international incident that was quickly quelled by high-level U.S. diplomacy. The Mexican government was none too happy to have U.S. military hardware raining down upon its northwestern territories, but diplomats quickly resolved the dispute.

Pershing Missile Similar to One That Crashed Near Coyame in 1967 (U.S. Army Photo)

The people of Coyame had even fresher memories of the July 11, 1970 crash of a 16,000-pound Athena intercontinental ballistic missile containing a small amount of radioactive material. The ICBM slammed into a mountainous desert area near Ceballos,

Durango – less than 200 miles from Coyame. Mexican ranchers discovered a large debris field described as "chunks of metal … scattered across the desert." This second major missile crash in a three-year period further increased tensions between the U.S. and Mexico. An American decontamination team worked for months at the Athena crash site to clean up residual radiation from the crash, in order to satisfy the Mexican government.

Within the context of these U.S. missile crashes, one can better understand why the events of August 25, 1974 did not cause the people of Coyame undue alarm or surprise. Perhaps this also explains why area residents were not particularly interested in trudging out to the middle of the desert at night, only to possibly encounter the radioactive remains of a downed U.S. missile.

The slow and painstaking search for eyewitnesses thus continues. If Jorge González is correct, the Coyame crash site was somewhere in the area of the *El Llano*, which in 1974 was extremely remote and virtually unpopulated. Someone may have seen or heard something that night. Perhaps those persons have since died or moved elsewhere. Or perhaps they are biding their time, waiting for an opportune moment to come forward with their amazing tale.

The full impact of the Coyame event will probably not be felt by society until a credible witness finally steps forward with important revelations. "This case is not yet closed," says Gilberto E. Rivera Altamirano, director of GIFAE in Chihuahua. "Witnesses and evidence are yet to be brought forth that will establish this case as a real historical event, comparable in scope to the July 1947 UFO crash near Roswell, New Mexico."

14. THE 2007 FIELD INVESTIGATION

During the first week of January 2007, authors Noe Torres and Ruben Uriarte traveled to the remote Chihuahuan desert town of Coyame, Mexico, bent on further unraveling the tantalizing mystery of the UFO crash in 1974. Packed in the bags of our Coyame investigative team were a wide range of digital video and audio recording equipment, as well as a global positioning receiver, handheld computers, and metal detector.

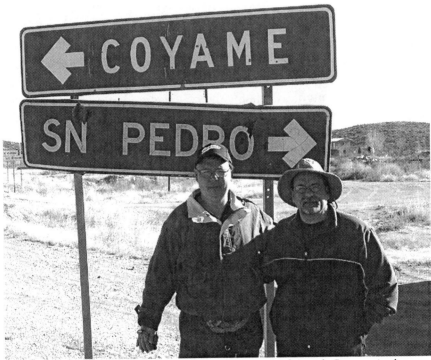

Authors Noe Torres (left) and Ruben Uriarte (right) with Coyame in the Background During January 2007 Visit

Before leaving for Coyame, we prepared for our field investigation by carefully reviewing information we had previously received from several individuals, including Mexican UFO investigator Gilberto Rivera, Coyame ranch owner Jorge González,

86

and Coyame resident Javier Baeza. We constructed a database of individuals that we very much desired to interview and of places we wanted to visit. Of greatest interest to our team was exploration of the area known as *El Llano*, located north-northeast of Coyame. Both González and Rivera were convinced that the 1974 crash likely occurred in the *El Llano* area.

Coyame Public Library (2006 by Ruben Uriarte)

Our guide and driver for the Coyame field investigation was Martin Sanchez Orozco, owner of a company in Chihuahua called Safari Aventura (*www.safariaventura.com.mx*), which specializes in outdoor adventure tourism such as hiking, biking, and canoeing. Sanchez is also intrigued by the paranormal and regularly takes tourists into Mexico's mysterious *Zone of Silence*. Although he was hired chiefly to handle the logistics of transporting us to where we needed to go, Sanchez soon proved his mettle as a field investigator, going way beyond the call of duty and making several important contributions to our investigation.

Upon arriving in on Wednesday, January 3, 2007, Sanchez suggested that we make contact with an acquaintance of his, Coyame's former sheriff, Filemon Cervantes, who lives a short distance from the town's central plaza and its small public library. Cervantes made two key early contributions to the team's investigation by: (1) providing the names of a number of local residents who might have information about this strange event, and (2) giving Martin Sanchez detailed information on how to navigate the dirt roads that connect Coyame with the many isolated ranches that stretch out for hundreds of miles across the harsh desert.

Cervantes, the former Coyame lawman, then took us on a driving tour around town, introducing us to several of the town's residents, all of whom became key players in our investigation. One of our first stops on the tour was the public library, just a short walk away from the town's center. Although the library was still closed due to the Christmas holidays, Cervantes took us to the house of librarian Yesenia Franco Muniz, who quickly agreed to give us an impromptu, private tour of the facility.

Coyame Librarian Yesenia Franco (right) with Author Noe Torres (2007 by Ruben Uriarte)

Ms. Franco became a valuable resource person to us regarding the history of the area and its people. She also warmly provided us access to the library's four brand new Windows XP computer workstations. Using one of the library's computers, we gave a short PowerPoint presentation about the 1974 Coyame UFO crash to a small group of assembled local residents and then also showed them excerpts from the December 2005 *History Channel* program titled "Mexico's Roswell." An eerie silence fell on the group as images of the UFO incident flickered onto the computer screen in front of us, as we realized that the marvelous events being described on the screen had occurred so near to the very place where we sat huddled on this cold January day in 2007.

Former sheriff Cervantes next took us to the home of Soledad "Soly" Bryant, a native of Coyame who is married to John Bryant of Hobbs, New Mexico. John, an oilfield worker in New Mexico, spends most of his time in Hobbs, where the couple's two children attend school. He visits his wife in Coyame whenever his schedule allows and also brings the kids when school holidays permit. It's about a 350-mile trip each way between Hobbs and Coyame, but the family seems to have adjusted.

Both Soly and John, a former U.S. Marine, are very interested in the 1974 Coyame UFO case. According to Soly, she first heard about the case when her husband ran across a copy of the Deneb report on the Internet in New Mexico and faxed a copy of it to her in Coyame. Coincidentally, very shortly after receiving the report from her husband, Soly was contacted by a reporter for the *History Channel* and was interviewed about the case for the 2005 *UFO Files* program.

Soly admits that since the day she first heard about the case, she has been greatly interested in finding out more details about it. Until recently, her ability to investigate further was hampered by the need to care for her ailing mother, who passed away in December 2006. Now, she desires to spend more time checking around the Coyame area, looking for clues about the mysterious happenings of August 1974.

While our team of investigators was in Coyame, Soly's continued interest in the case led us to the discovery of two very interesting sites in the desert north of town, as will be discussed in later chapters of this book. "It's an amazing story," Soly told the authors. "When my husband first told me about it, I couldn't believe that something like this had happened right here in Coyame!"

Our Coyame investigative team also talked to a number of area residents who have witnessed strange objects streaking across the sky at night, followed by explosions. A group of Mexican soldiers, manning a drug checkpoint just east of Coyame, pointed up into the sky over the mountain ranges to the north as they described strange objects that blazed across the night sky, illuminating the mountains below before apparently slamming into the earth miles away from them.

Coyame's secretary for tourism, Santa Isabel Ramirez Aguilar, during an interview with the authors, said that she does not understand why local journalists do not print more stories about the unusual events that frequently happen in the Coyame area. "Local residents recently saw what seemed to be a large meteorite thundering across the sky and falling with a great explosion that shook the earth," Ramirez said, "But nobody seems too interested in reporting these sorts of events."

Santa Isabel Ramirez Aguilar, Coyame Secretary for Tourism (2007 by Ruben Uriarte)

In a meeting with Mrs. Ramirez and other members of the city hall staff, the authors of this book presented information about the

1974 Coyame UFO event and answered a number of questions from the municipal employees about the case. According to Mrs. Ramirez, some local residents, after hearing reports about it on Mexican television in the past year, had the mistaken notion that the event must have occurred within the town of Coyame itself. She listened attentively, nodding in agreement, as we explained that our evidence suggests the crash occurred a good distance (perhaps 50 miles or more) outside of town.

Following our visit to city hall, we had a meal at the town's lone restaurant, *La Estrella*, whose owner, Elizabeth Rodriguez Armendariz, entertained us with stories of residents who have seen flying objects and other strange apparitions in the area. She told us an eerie tale of "wind volcanoes," a frightening phenomenon that has been witnessed by several persons in the Coyame area. These are apertures in the ground that suddenly emit strong bursts of a gusty vapor up into the atmosphere.

There seemed little doubt that, for whatever reason, the Coyame area is home to a great deal of paranormal activity. Contributing to a strong feeling of eeriness are the surrounding desert landscape, the sense of isolation, and the realization that, if the 1974 UFO event can be proven beyond doubt, this seemingly insignificant Mexican desert town will take a prominent place in the annals of human history.

15. Seeking The Crash Site

Most UFO investigators favor a crash site between 25 and 50 air miles north-northeast of Coyame, in or near the area known as *El Llano*. Other researchers have suggested that the UFO-airplane collision might have taken place southeast of Coyame, perhaps as much as 50 miles from town center. Nonetheless, the evidence uncovered during the writing of this book leads the authors to conclude that an *El Llano* crash location best fits the available facts.

According to the Deneb report, the U.S. helicopters left El Paso on August 26, 1974 and moved south along the Rio Grande River, entering Mexican airspace at a point just north of the tiny Texas town of Candelaria. Just before arriving over Candelaria, the copters veered into Mexico and arrived quickly at the scene of the Mexican convoy's final resting place in the desert. This information suggests that the crash retrieval by the U.S. forces occurred a short distance west or southwest of Candelaria.

If the helicopters' destination had been farther north than Candelaria, they would have entered into Mexico earlier, and if their destination were farther south, they would have entered later, perhaps closer to Presidio, Texas or Redford, Texas. It seems, therefore, that the copters were headed not far from Candelaria, suggesting a location north-northeast of Coyame.

The Deneb report states, "It was not until 1438 hrs that the helicopters departed Ft. Bliss. The four helicopters followed the border down towards Presidio then turned and entered Mexican airspace north of Candelaria. They were over the convoy site at 1653 hrs." The total flight time was two hours and 15 minutes.

The slowest of the helicopters, the UH-1 Huey, typically cruises (at sea level) at about 140 miles per hour; however, due to the mountainous terrain and higher elevation, the flight speed may have averaged closer to 100 m.p.h. Using this speed estimate, the total distance flown from Fort Bliss (latitude 31.8, latitude –106.42) to the UFO site was approximately 225 miles. Since the distance from Fort Bliss to Candelaria (latitude 30.138, longitude –104.685) is 154 air miles, the helicopters probably flew about 71 additional miles after making the turn into Mexico. The distance in air miles from Candelaria to Coyame is 52.1. The distance from Candelaria to Rancho El Llano is 29.42 air miles.

It is unlikely that the U.S. helicopters would have turned back north after entering Mexico near Candelaria. Therefore, it seems that their destination was the area immediately west of Candelaria, extending up to 71 miles from the Rio Grande River. In the map that follows, we have drawn a shaded circle where most researchers feel the crash and recovery occurred. The map also displays an arrow where the U.S. helicopters first entered Mexican air space.

Not far from the center of this shaded area, toward the northeast, is Rancho El Llano, located 38 air miles from the town of Coyame, which lies southwest of it. This ranch is located in the midst of a vast expanse of plain known as *El Llano*.

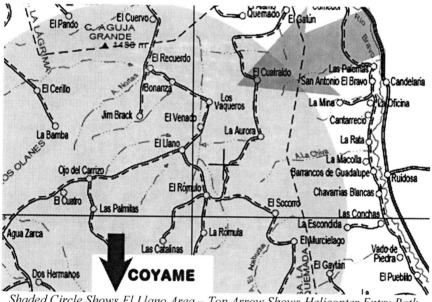

Shaded Circle Shows El Llano Area – Top Arrow Shows Helicopter Entry Path. Bottom Arrow Points Toward Coyame, Which is About 30 miles to the South

On January 4, 2007, the authors and their investigative team began investigating along the 60-mile stretch of graded, unpaved road between Coyame and *El Llano*, seeking any available corroboration for the August 1974 event. Although *El Llano* is only about 38 miles from Coyame by air, the only road connecting these two points is a long, rugged loop that serves to link many of the local ranches to the federal highway that runs through Coyame. This rough road, which the locals refer to as *La Brecha* ("the breach"), is flanked on both sides by deep ditches. Under the best of weather conditions, it makes for a difficult and bumpy drive that is best navigated with a four-wheel drive vehicle. After a good rainfall, the road becomes virtually impassible in many areas. Although we did not have four-wheel drive, our guide Martin Sanchez assured us that his trusty 1993 GMC Suburban sport utility vehicle was more than up to the task of navigating *La Brecha*.

Dirt Road Called "La Brecha" Winds 60 miles from Coyame to El Llano
(2007 by Ruben Uriarte)

Before leaving Coyame, our group received explicit instructions from Filemon Cervantes, former sheriff of the town, on how to make the long drive out to *El Llano*. Cervantes cautioned our guide, Martin Sanchez, to stay close to the center of *La Brecha* and to avoid accidentally taking one of the many unmarked minor roads that split off from the main road. He also recited the names of the major ranches that we would pass close to on our way to our destination.

"There are many, many small ranches all around *El Llano*," Cervantes told us. "On the way there, be sure to stay on the main road, *La Brecha*, which actually goes all the way beyond *El Llano* to the Rio Grande River."

He explained that *La Brecha* functions as a dirt "highway," from which many smaller roads branch off, all of them leading to the various ranches in the area. "If you accidentally end up at one of the ranches, just ask the people there to help you get back to the main road," Cervantes added helpfully.

Interestingly, Cervantes also pointed out that this primitive desert road system also included branches that led directly from near *El Llano* to Chihuahua City and also back down to Highway 16 near Ojinaga. The ranchers and ranch workers use these dirt roads to travel to Chihuahua or Ojinaga without having to come down to Coyame.

Following the UFO crash in 1974, the Mexican military units responsible for recovering the crash debris would have had no trouble whatsoever navigating the desert expanse north and northeast of Coyame using this elaborate system of back roads. A vast military armada could easily make its way across the desert to carry out the crash retrieval with very little chance of being interfered with or even detected.

The military presence in this area is commonplace, and few local residents ask any questions when they see troop movements and military vehicles. Although our investigative team was in Coyame only a few days, we saw a number of military troop movements in the area, including a sighting of a Mexican army jeep carrying soldiers near *El Llano*. Local residents told us that all of these army units are dispatched out of the base at Ojinaga.

After former sheriff Cervantes set our party on the right path, we began our journey out of the small town of Coyame, headed north toward *El Llano* in our GMC Suburban. As we exited the town's northwest quadrant, we passed Coyame's quaint baseball stadium, void of grass but otherwise attractive and well designed. We later discovered, during a visit to the municipal building, that Coyame fielded outstanding semi-pro baseball teams in the 1950s. A local team called "Red Fury" carries the tradition forward, competing against teams from neighboring towns.

Across the dirt road from the baseball park is the small municipal cemetery with its mostly simple and functional grave markers. The small size of the cemetery bears testimony to the fact that Coyame has always been sparsely populated.

95

16. A MYSTERIOUS HOLE IN THE GROUND

About five miles from Coyame's town center is a very strange site indeed, to which we were taken by a group of local residents led by Soly Bryant and her uncle, Leandro Valeriano. At this location is a circle of blackened dirt at the center of which is a deep hole in the ground marked off by wooden beams. The site is surrounded by a hastily assembled barbed wire fence that has partly fallen, and the entire area is littered with rusted metal debris from various vehicles, such as coils, springs, gauges, and metal bars.

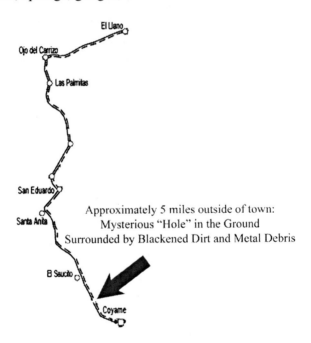

Approximately 5 miles outside of town:
Mysterious "Hole" in the Ground
Surrounded by Blackened Dirt and Metal Debris

Valeriano, who had been out to the site before, expresses uncertainty as to what its purpose was. He guesses that somebody brought in machinery to dig the hole but that the project was abandoned for some unknown reason. He is at a loss to explain the presence of numerous rusted metal parts all around the site. Several members of our team speculated that the hole in the ground might have been used as a waste dump, into which people later threw various pieces of metal and car parts.

Valeriano also cannot explain the blackened soil all around the site, which seemed to indicate fire or explosion at some point in the past. The evidence of burning did not seem recent, as the blackening of the soil had faded considerably with time. According to Valeriano, the property on which the hole is located has been unoccupied and for sale for at least ten years. He did not know where the former owner is.

A Mysterious Hole in the Desert Surrounded by Blackened Dirt and Metal Debris
(2007 by Ruben Uriarte)

"They may have begun digging a well for water here," Valeriano said, "and then for some reason, they couldn't finish it. It doesn't look like it's been used for dumping trash, but there's all these pieces of metal all around here, and the dirt looks like it was burned some time ago."

Among the more interesting items that we retrieved at this site was a water pressure gauge of some sort, perhaps from a truck or other vehicle. Unfortunately, it does not contain very much information on it that might prove useful for identifying it. John and Soly Bryant had previously collected the piece near the mysterious hole in the ground, and they showed it to us on the day that they took us out to look at the site. Their immediate thought was that this gauge might have come from one of the Mexican jeeps or trucks that, according to the Deneb report, was exploded by the U.S. soldiers right before they left the area and took the recovered UFO back to Texas.

"It's really hard to say for sure where this comes from," we later were told by a source familiar with military vehicles. "If it is from some kind of vehicle, it could be from a jeep, a truck, a tractor, a caterpillar, or something else."

Water Temperature Gauge Found Near Coyame (2007 by Noe Torres)

We also found other metal springs and rods that could conceivably have come from aircraft, but they are too generic looking to know for sure, and they contained no serial numbers or other markings that could help identify them. "To me, some of these look like airplane parts," said Soly Bryant.

After exploring the site with a metal detector, taking many photographs, and talking with Valeriano and the Bryants, we concluded our investigation of the mysterious hole in the desert near Coyame. Our conclusion was that it would be very interesting to conduct an excavation of the hole to find out what might be buried down below the ground.

What Secrets Lie Buried Inside This Hole? (2007 by Ruben Uriarte)

17. The Airplane Crash Debris

Coyame resident Leandro Valeriano, the uncle of Soly Bryant, next took us to another even more thought-provoking site, located along *La Brecha* another mile beyond the mysterious hole in the ground. Valeriano had a vague memory of a small airplane crash that had occurred in this general area many years previously. The story that authorities told the local townspeople was that a drug trafficker was piloting a light aircraft at a very low altitude when the plane clipped the top of a mountain and went down in the desert.

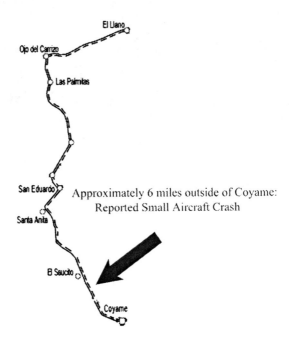

Approximately 6 miles outside of Coyame: Reported Small Aircraft Crash

"It happened about twenty years ago," Valeriano said, which would have meant that the crash occurred sometime around 1986, as far as the locals can remember. "The authorities showed up and removed several truckloads of debris. The funny thing about it was that the pilot's body was never found. All they ever found was one human arm."

Valeriano said that government officials cordoned off the area of the crash, and no civilians were allowed to get close to it. "Everything was all burned up," He added. "The fire continued for several days. It was so hot that some parts of the plane melted down into pools of molten metal." Later, there were rumors that fragments of burned paper currency had been found scattered all over the area, but it was believed that none of the bills were intact.

Even though the approximate1986 time frame did not fit with the 1974 UFO event, the idea of finding airplane crash debris near Coyame was very intriguing to our investigative team. It would help us in several ways. First, it would identify and isolate this unrelated plane crash from the 1974 event. This was important because we had previously heard local residents talking about a plane crash in the mid to late 1980s. Second, finding debris from this seemingly unrelated plane crash would suggest that it might still be possible to also find debris from the 1974 crash.

Relying on Valeriano's memories as to the location of the plane crash, we scoured the surrounding desert for about an hour but were unable to locate any evidence of a crash. "It's been so many years," Valeriano said, apologetically. "It's hard to find things after so many years have passed."

Scanning the surrounding brush and rocks, Valeriano added, "Besides, as I recall, most of the wreckage was removed from here by the authorities. And then, people came and took the rest to sell as scrap metal. I don't think there would be much left here now."

Moments after he made this statement, we noticed that our guide Martin Sanchez was searching an area several hundred feet away from where Valeriano had suggested that we look. Valeriano saw him and called out, "No, it's not over there. That's too far away. Come over this way. This way."

Suddenly, Sanchez stood up from a crouching position and held up high over his head an assembly consisting of rusty metal tubes. We realized that Sanchez had located the airplane crash debris that had thus far eluded the other members of our team. As we all raced to where Sanchez was, the object he was holding above his head became clearer to us. Later, a source familiar with military aircraft, told us that the structure might be a portion of a horizontal stabilizer bar or rudder.

Within moments, we reached the area where Sanchez had found the strange artifact. We immediately noticed on the ground all around us numerous pieces of metal, including lots of aluminum, confirming that we had indeed found the site of an airplane crash. We quickly set us upon the task of trying to find pieces that contained serial numbers, the names of manufacturers, or any other identifying information.

Valeriano Examines Part of the Wreckage Found (2007 by Ruben Uriarte)

Although we knew it was unlikely that this crash had anything to do with the 1974 UFO case, it nonetheless produced heart-pumping excitement among the members of our investigative group. It was one of those *Wow* moments that field researchers dream about – to actually stumble across the very thing that you are hoping to find in the very place that you heard something happened.

Following the discovery, we took copious photographs, bagged a few of the parts to take back with us for possible identification, and then held a brief, impromptu celebration in the desert. Toasting each other with lukewarm coffee made by our guide earlier in the day, we stood alongside *La Brecha* and congratulated ourselves on a most significant find. It was not exactly what we were looking for, but it was a start, and it was also a lot more than any previous investigators had found.

Later, after we had returned to the United States, the pieces of the wreckage were shown to several Air Force pilots. The aviators were able to identify one of the pieces as belonging to the extend-retract linkages of the landing gear of a light aircraft. This indicates that the wreckage was of a single or dual engine light aircraft with retractable, rather than fixed, landing gear. The exact type of plane could not be ascertained from the wreckage collected, but it could have been something like a Beechcraft Bonanza or Mooney Acclaim.

Some of the Plane Wreckage Found (2007 by Ruben Uriarte)

The plight of this supposed drug trafficking plane also brings to the forefront another interesting theory about the 1974 UFO crash event. Some observers have wondered if the light aircraft mentioned in the 1974 collision with the UFO might also have been involved in drug smuggling or other illegal activities. If this were the case, it would explain why very little information has surfaced about the plane and its occupant or occupants. The Mexican-registered plane, bound from El Paso to Mexico City, was apparently never reported lost, nor have any documents ever been found in which its flight is even noted.

18. Exploring *El Llano*

Initally, a principal objective of our Coyame investigation was to explore the area known as *El Llano*, which is where many researchers feel the 1974 UFO crash retrieval occurred. With this objective still clearly in mind, our team ventured farther north along *La Brecha*, making our way slowly toward our planned destination. Along the way, we passed many smaller roads leading to area ranches, with many of the roads being marked by signs put up by the local cattleman's association.

Authors Noe Torres and Ruben Uriarte in Front of Sign Listing Ranches Located Near El Llano (2007 by Martin Sanchez)

As we made our way closer to *El Llano*, we came upon several unusual twists in the road and a couple of unmarked intersections. Consequently, as we approached a ranch called *Ejido El Carrizo*, we were not completely certain whether we were still on the right course. As fate would have it, our driver Martin Sanchez decided to venture away from the main road and try to find someone in a nearby ranch to help us find our way. Sanchez also wanted to borrow some tools from someone in order to fix an electrical switch inside his dashboard assembly that had failed, causing the sport utility vehicle's headlights not to work. Since it was doubtful that we would get back to Coyame before nightfall, Sanchez did not want to have to drive the dark desert back roads without headlights.

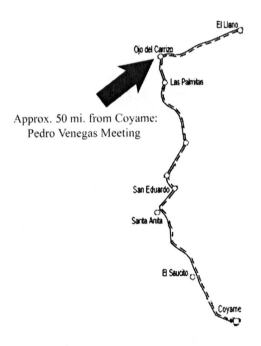

Approx. 50 mi. from Coyame:
Pedro Venegas Meeting

The first ranch we wandered into was *El Carrizo*, which at first seemed totally abandoned. A number of dilapidated buildings, including a schoolhouse, bore testimony to a bygone era, but there seemed to be not a soul around. As we were about to leave, we noticed an elderly gentleman wearing a cowboy hat and a blue-jean jacket coming out of one of the small houses in the ranch.

The man turned out to be Pedro Venegas Leyva, who has been tending livestock on this ranch for many years. When we explained who we were and what our investigation was about, he immediately became very quiet and attentive. Although he had never heard of the 1974 Coyame UFO event, he told us that he remembered an incident "at around that time" when the quiet ranch was suddenly shaken by two loud explosions. The explosions caused the windows of his ranch house to rattle. Unfortunately, he could not tell us the exact date of the explosions, and he had no other information about anything else from that time period.

Rancho El Carrizo (2007 by Ruben Uriarte)

About the strangeness of the *El Llano* area, he did have a lot more to say, however. He invited us into his home and showed us his notes about to very unusual sightings of unidentified aircraft that he personally had.

His first sighting occurred on Saturday, January 20, 1996 at 1:30 a.m. Standing outside his house in *El Carrizo* and looking to the north, he saw a fast moving object streaking across the sky in an arc from west to east. The sky was cloudless, and the wind was still. Oval in shape, the object alternated in color from yellow to white to blue to clear. As it zoomed out of sight to the east, a thunderous noise shook the ground and rattled the Venegas home. The event made such an impression on him that he later wrote down careful notes describing what he had witnessed.

Venegas had a second sighting on Thursday, July 17, 1997 at 5 a.m. An object "like an aircraft" streaked across the sky from east to west, brightly illuminating the landscape below it. Like the earlier sighting, this one left Venegas fearful and wondering about the significance of these strange apparitions in the night sky.

After explaining to him that we were heading on toward *El Llano*, he graciously offered to accompany us for the remaining twenty miles or so. Joining us in our SUV, Venegas continued to provide us with a wealth of information about *El Llano* and the many ranches that dot the area. He pointed out to us that we were actually very near to the Rio Grande River, which was just beyond a vast mountain range that dominated the landscape ahead of us to the east. "Just beyond those mountains and a little to the north lies the town of Candelaria, Texas," he told us.

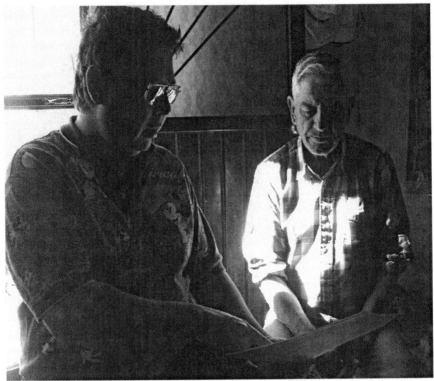

Noe Torres (left) Speaks With Pedro Venegas (2007 by Ruben Uriarte)

The team members looked at one another. "This is right where the U.S. helicopters flew on their way to recover the crashed UFO," someone noted, as others nodded in agreement.

With navigational help from Venegas, we arrived quickly onto the immense plain known as *El Llano*, and although there are many ranches scattered throughout this area, unfortunately the day was waning, and we would only be able to visit one more ranch today. Still facing the 60-mile return trip to Coyame along the same very rugged dirt road by which we came, we wrapped up our visit to this mysterious land with a quick chat with one of the owners of the

Rancho El Llano, Salome Baeza.

Baeza had been just a child in 1974, but he told us that he never heard his father, or anyone else, mention anything related to a plane crash or UFO sighting in 1974. He did admit, however, that the persons most likely to have heard or seen something would be the ranch hands, the majority of whom are poor, illiterate transients. The ranch owners and managers often spend little time at the ranches, opting for the comfort of their permanent residences in nearby cities like Chihuahua and Ojinaga. The ranch hands, often drawn from indigenous populations such as the Tarahumara Indians of the Copper Canyon region, tend to move frequently from ranch to ranch.

"Beyond Those Mountains is Candelaria" -- Pedro Venegas (2007 by Ruben Uriarte)

Heading back along *La Brecha* back toward Coyame, we were struck by the massiveness of the task that still lay before us in the future. It was clear that to find more evidence of the 1974 Coyame crash retrieval would take many, many years of careful and methodical searching of all the ranches in this area. Or perhaps one day, just as we stumbled upon the wreckage of the drug trafficking airplane, someone may just happen across the very proof that we ourselves had hoped by chance to find during our brief visit.

19. ZONE OF SILENCE

Before colliding with the aircraft somewhere north of Coyame, the UFO traversed the skies over Coahuila state, passing directly over a very strange region of Mexico known as *La Zona del Silencio*, the Zone of Silence. Located about 400 miles southeast of El Paso, the area got its name from the strange natural phenomena that have been observed there over the years. In addition to numerous sightings of UFOs and mysterious beings, the area is said to generate mysterious waves of electromagnetic energy that can disrupt radios, telephones, aircraft instruments, and other electronic devices.

Ruben Uriarte Stands on the Road to the Zone of Silence in October 2006

The first recorded instance of the Zone of Silence affecting an aircraft in flight occurred in the 1930s. While flying over the zone, legendary Mexican aviator Francisco Sarabia reported that his radio ceased to function. But the incident that really put the Zone on the map was the crash of a U.S. intercontinental ballistic missile, carrying a small amount of radioactive material on July 11, 1970. The missile flew hundreds of miles off course and slammed directly into the middle of the Zone.

The Athena ICBM, carrying a small amount of radioactive Cobalt 57, was fired from Green River, Utah, and crashed in the desert near Ceballos, Durango, Mexico, about 200 miles south of the Texas border. Two days after the crash, local ranchers found a debris field near Ceballos, where "chunks of metal were scattered across the desert."

A Marker Points to Where an Athena ICBM Crashed (2006 By Ruben Uriarte)

The nose cone containing the radioactive Cobalt 57 was finally located on August 2 by a special U.S. recovery team dispatched to the area. The team found a small crater area with just a few pieces of twisted metal and some contaminated sand. The recovery crew detected only a very low level of radioactivity at the site.

Like the Bermuda Triangle and other similarly mysterious regions of the earth, Mexico's Zone of Silence is located between the Tropic of Cancer and the 30th parallel. Researchers have expressed scientific curiosity about the area's natural and electromagnetic properties, while psychic investigators have suggested the Zone may be a "gateway" linking our world with other dimensions.

During a 2006 visit to the Zone of Silence, co-author Ruben

Uriarte was amazed at the amount of animal life and vegetation that he saw. "What surprised me about traveling to La Zona del Silencio is that the desert is a very fertile area, the Garden of Eden as a friend of mine once described it." The Zone is a true natural biosphere where plant and animal life are sustained in a delicately balanced environment. The area's life is sustained by nature's gifts of water, sun and other natural elements. This immense area stretches over 200 miles and takes in parts of three Mexican states -- Chihuahua, Durango and Coahuila.

"I noticed that there were many settlements of people encroaching upon the land and living off its resources," Uriarte wrote in a journal kept during his visit. "Although it is arid, the area appears to have water from underwater aquifers and other sources."

In the Zone of Silence (2006 By Ruben Uriarte)

"We went at a good time, when the weather was cool during the day and very cold at night. One day, we were hit by stormy weather with heavy rain, lightning, and powerful winds. While the storm was beautiful in a way, it was also scary for us, because we were so far off the beaten path."

"After the rain subsided, I noticed that the desert seemed green and alive. Also, following these heavy downpours, we had to drive very carefully so that our truck would not get stuck in mud or suddenly caught in a flash flood."

The experience of entering the Zone of Silence reminded the authors of being on safari in a vast African prairie, such as is often portrayed on television and in motion pictures. It was an awe-inspiring site to see the vastness of the desert spread before us like a blanket.

During our visit, we struck camp at an abandoned hacienda called *Hacienda de los Remedios*, or the "Place of Healing." Originally built in 1906 as a place where people could come to be "treated" for various illnesses by bathing in the warm thermal water that bubbles up here from underground springs. The water is said to have miraculous healing properties.

Hacienda de los Remedios (2006 By Ruben Uriarte)

"We were hit by a powerful storm at our campsite, and our tents and sleeping bag gear got very wet," Uriarte wrote in his journal. "We were very cold, but we loved the warmth of the water from the hot springs. In a nearby cave, we found a pool of very warm water with a waterfall at one end. The source of the water was somewhere deep underground. A system of pipes directs the water to several outdoor pools and to an irrigation system. The water, although rich in minerals, has no discernable bad odor, such as that of sulfur."

"The waterfall was like a powerful shower of warm water, and it felt great to be soaked by it. I used a light stick to illuminate one of the cavern walls and found that its surface was covered with sparkling crystals of some sort. This gave me the feeling that I was in a crystal temple and that great energy was flowing into my body from the warm, healing waters springing up from the earth. The locals come here to this very spot to bathe and relax. I felt very blessed."

While traveling in the Zone, the authors saw a great variety of bushes, trees, cacti, and strange rock formations. In addition to the occasional tarantula or other desert dweller, we noticed stalks of corn growing wild alongside the roads there. "I found it strange that corn was growing in a desert area, but it demonstrates how fertile this barren landscape actually is. Those wild corn plants probably date back to the time of Mexican revolution, when many poor people were given portions of land to farm."

Today, corn grown in the Zone of Silence is used to make tortillas for the local population. Ranches in the area also raise cattle and other livestock. A few very small stores are scattered throughout the area, providing cold refreshments, food items, and bare necessities.

In a small village within the Zone, we found a "salt farm," where salt is collected in special ponds by an evaporative technique. He also found seashells that suggest the area was once part of an ancient sea, perhaps thousands or even millions of years ago. Local people say that many fossils of ancient sea life have been found here as well.

In the Zone of Silence (2006 By Ruben Uriarte)

We also came across an abandoned mercury mine that was closed down many years ago. Its presence reminds us that, despite its appearance as a desert wasteland, the Zone contains essential natural resources that have enabled human and wildlife to survive here for many years in otherwise bleak conditions.

At one point in our travels, we witnessed a thundering noise and massive cloud of dust heading our way. With a certain amount of trepidation, we waited anxiously within the safe confines of our truck. The dust cleared somewhat as the monster approached, revealing a massive herd of wild horses that shook the ground and our vehicle as they thundered past us, just a short distance away.

As visitors explore the Zone of Silence, they are often met with glares from the poor farmers and ranchers of the area. Protective of their little parcels of government-granted land, known as *ejidos*, the locals are not happy to see strangers stomping across their fields. Sometimes the farmers will confront outsiders and turn them away, much to the chagrin of tourism promoters. The promoters know that if the locals were more open to visitors, tourism would increase, bringing much needed additional revenue to the area.

The tour guide for our party, Martin Sanchez, made it a practice to stop in at the various *ejidos* to speak with key people about his tour business. He explained to them that tourists help boost the local economy and expressed his desire to work closely with each *ejido* to facilitate the flow of visitors through the area.

We stopped and took pictures of numerous rock formations and mountain ranges. Some of the local peaks and rock formations are named after people. Apparently a man named Uribe once owned a large portion of the Zone, as a number of natural features are named after members of his family. His wife, Juana, is immortalized by twin peaks known as "the breasts of Juana." The locals still tell the story of how the naming of the peaks was an apt tribute to a woman who was very amply endowed at the chest.

After briefly visiting the crash site of the Athena rocket fell near Ceballos, Durango, on July 11, 1970, we drove on to the Mapimi Biosphere Reserve, an ecological laboratory operated by the state of Durango, located within the massive Chihuahuan desert, which covers a large part of northern Mexico before ambling into Texas, New Mexico, and Arizona. The area is noted for its unique floral and fauna species and for a particular type of tortoise that is found only here. Many scientist and university students come to the laboratory to study the ecology, geology and other aspects of the environment.

Researchers at the Mapimi reserve are generally annoyed by tourists, who are viewed as interfering with their work. Writer Andrea Kaus of the ecotourism Web site *Planeta.com* states, "The Mapimi Reserve overlaps an area known as La Zona del Silencio (the Zone of Silence) which attracts tourists and curiosity-seekers from all over the world. These people and their guides are locally referred to as *zoneros* or *silenciosos*. They are generally considered to be slightly daft or a nuisance, but they represent a substantial population of strangers who wish to see, experience, and take away with them a memento of what they perceive to be the strange essence of the Mapimian desert."

Joining us on our trip was paranormal investigator Victor Camacho, host of the popular Spanish-language program *Los Desvelados*. As we traveled, we asked people along the way if they had encountered anything "out of the ordinary" in the Zone of Silence. As this area has been a hotbed of UFO activity and other paranormal anomalies, we hoped to hear a few good tales. However, it was our experience that the local people tend to keep to themselves and shy away from outsiders. Nonetheless, the authors are convinced that, given enough time to explore the area and get to know some of the people, some remarkable tales would surely have emerged.

20. DEATH FROM THE SKY

One of the unique aspects of the Coyame story is that an unknown substance at the crash site caused the deaths of perhaps as many as two-dozen soldiers. Even as they succumbed to the mysterious and invisible chemical or biological agent, they apparently remained totally unaware of its cause. The presence of this deadly agent motivated a U.S. military task force to rush into Mexico and set off an incendiary device, possibly nuclear, to prevent any further spread of the problem. Although the massive explosion obliterated most physical clues regarding the causal agent, many questions linger about the risks associated with deadly extraterrestrial contaminants being introduced into our environment as a result of a UFO encounter.

Many "close encounter" UFO cases over the years have resulted in the human observers receiving injuries such as radiation sickness, burns, paralysis, blindness, and numbness. According to *The Encyclopedia of UFOs*, sightings typically carry a risk of exposure to perhaps four kilorads of radiation. Although there have been cases where the UFO eyewitnesses have grown very ill following a sighting, deaths resulting from a close encounter have been extremely rare.

A number of UFO-related deaths involve pilots whose airplanes crashed while pursuing a UFO. In a few rare cases, witnesses have dropped dead of unknown causes shortly after encountering a UFO. According to the *Fire Officer's Guide to Disaster Control*, "While pursuing UFOs, military aircraft have disappeared in mid-air, exploded, and suffered harassment. Persons on the ground have sustained serious burns, paralysis, and 'blows' from a force field, radiated emissions, or rays and beams that have been described like that of a 'stun-gun.'"

Beginning in the late 1970s, UFOs were blamed for numerous burn cases among the indigenous populations living along the Amazon River in Brazil. Eyewitnesses described flying discs hovering above residences, emitting beams of red light that penetrated the roofs of houses and burned the persons within. In

1993, a Brazilian doctor said she treated more than 40 villagers for strange burns and knew of at least two deaths resulting from the reported UFO encounters.

In its famous chapter on UFOs, the 1992 edition of *Fire Officer's Guide to Disaster Control* carries the following admonition: "Near approaches of UFOs can be harmful to human beings. Do not stand under a UFO that is hovering at low altitude. Do not touch or attempt to touch a UFO that has landed. In either case the safe thing to do is to get away from there very quickly and let the military take over. There is a possibility of radiation danger and there are known cases where persons have been burned by rays emanating from UFOs. Don't take chances with UFOs!"

The Coyame case is unusual in the sense that contact with a crashed UFO resulted in the deaths of perhaps as many as 24 human beings. The deaths were not likely the result of heat, radiation, or electromagnetic force. The deaths were probably the result of an invisible substance venting into the atmosphere around the crash site. Although the substance may have been biological or chemical, the actions of the U.S. task force indicates that the task force onsite seemed to believe it was biological and that it posed a grave danger to nearby populations.

The "Deneb report," which first disclosed the event, stated, "Unfortunately, what caused the deaths of the Mexican recovery team is not known. Speculation ranges from a chemical released from the disk, as a result of the damage, to a microbiological agent. There are no indications of death or illness by any of the [American] recovery team."

The concept that bacteria or viruses could travel to earth from outer space has been much discussed since the National Aeronautics Administration announced in 1996 that scientists had found evidence of a primitive form of microscopic life in a 4.5-billion-year-old meteorite that came to earth from Mars 13,000 years ago. Meteorite ALH 84001, found buried in Antarctica, was found to contain fossilized "nanobacteria" suggesting the possibility that life may have once existed on Mars.

The idea that the building blocks of life traveled through space and were responsible for the origin of life on earth is called *panspermia*. First proposed in the 5th Century BC by Greek philosopher Anaxagoras, the theory proposes that microbial life may have seeded life on earth after traveling to our planet on comets or meteors.

The airburst of a meteor may have deposited biological cell-like structures into the atmosphere over Kerala, India in 2001. According to an article by Louis Godfrey and A. Santhosh Kuamar in *Astrophysics and Space Science*, the deposited extraterrestrial biological material, containing carbon and oxygen, may have caused the strange "red rain" atmospheric phenomenon experienced in Kerala on July 25, 2001.

Martian Meteorite Said to Contain Evidence of Life (NASA)

Earth's own space travelers have already proven that DNA-based life can thrive in the rigors of outer space. In 1970, the astronauts of Apollo 12 brought back to earth a camera that had been deposited on the moon by an unmanned space probe in 1967. The camera was found to contain a colony of the bacterium *Streptococcus Mitis*, which had been deposited there when a technician sneezed on it prior to its 1967 launch. Amazingly, the bacteria survived the rocket launch, intense heat and radiation, crushing pressures, the vacuum of space, and the moon's freezing temperatures. Apollo 12 astronaut Pete Conrad called the bacteria "the most significant thing we found on the moon."

In addition to life traveling to earth on a meteor or comet, others have proposed that its introduction here on earth may have been a bit more deliberate. If UFOs visited the earth in our ancient history, panspermia takes on an entirely new twist. In that case, perhaps the seeding of life on earth was deliberate and scientific, rather than accidental and haphazard.

Until the Coyame information came to light, very little had been written about biological contamination of the earth from a UFO encounter. It is important to note that most scientists feel extraterrestrial viruses are unlikely to affect human beings, who would have entirely different DNA. Even within life on earth, interspecies transmission of diseases is extremely rare. Although human DNA may approximate some species of tree by as much as 70 percent, humans do not get tree diseases. Therefore, it seems unlikely that humans have much to fear from diseases that would affect totally alien DNA.

The exception, of course, would be an alien virus that was specifically engineered to affect human beings. It would certainly be within the suspected technology of UFO occupants to manufacture a deadly weaponized biological contaminant.

Until recently, no known historical documentation existed that linked UFO crash retrievals and biological warfare. According to UFO researcher Ryan S. Wood, a document that makes this connection surfaced at the Public Record Office in Kew, England. The one-page memo, dated 6 May 1950 and titled "Subject: Bacteriological Warfare Article," is a memo to the attention of the British Ministry of Defense's Scientific and Technical Intelligence Branch. The document suggests that officials within the British Ministry of Defense in the early 1950s might have at least thought about the possibility of weaponizing biological materials retrieved in a UFO crash.

Wood also cites an excerpt from a recently uncovered "Majestic 12" document that talks about the lethal contamination of four laboratory technicians who died after supposedly handling the debris and bodies from several UFO crash retrievals. The unverified *Majestic 12, 1st Annual Report* states that the SED (Sandia National

Laboratory) technicians died of seizures and profuse bleeding after coming into contact with both UFO crash debris and "body fluids from the occupants." Later, the report's author makes the chilling statement, "In the opinion of the senior AEC [Atomic Energy Commission] medical officer, current medical equipment and supplies are wholly inadequate in dealing with a large scale outbreak of the alien virus."

The Panel was concerned over the contamination of several SED personnel upon coming in contact with debris near the power plant. One technician was overcome and collapsed when he attempted the removal of a body. Another medical technician went into a coma four hours after placing a body in a rubber body-bag. All four were rushed to Los Alamos for observation. All four later died of seizures and profuse bleeding. All four were wearing protective suits when they came in contact with body fluids from the occupants.

Autopsies on the four dead SED technicians are not conclusive. It is believed that the four may have suffered from some form of toxin or a highly contagious disease. Tissue samples are currently being kept at Fort Detrick, Md.

Excerpt from Majestic 12, 1ˢᵗ Annual Report (majesticdocuments.com)

The U.S. military's action in detonating an incendiary device to cleanse the contaminated area near Coyame seems to indicate that a lethal biological agent was suspected. Once a biological infestation was suspected, the use of high explosives or a nuclear weapon came into play.

Regarding the use of a nuclear device, Paul Sutton, a U.S. military historian, said, "If the unknown lethal biological agent was of an off-planet origin, then maybe a small nuclear weapon would have been used. The U.S. had backpack nuclear weapons in the 1960s and 1970s called Atomic Demolition Munitions."

Sutton added that another type of explosive device might also have been used, "If the biological threat was from earth, then a fuel air explosive (FAE) might have been used to sterilize the area. An FAE uses a mist of fuel that is ignited in the air to destroy its target area."

In his eye-opening government-sponsored report, *Radiation-Neutralization of Stored Biological Warfare Agents with Low-Yield*

Nuclear Warheads, Hans Kruger argues that low-yield nuclear weapons are effective in neutralizing deadly biological agents. He wrote, "Nuclear explosions produce many effects that can potentially destroy a biological agent. These effects include blast overpressure, prompt radiation dose, fireball heat, and radiation dose from the delayed gammas and neutrons emitted by the fission debris cloud. The extent to which fireball heat and delayed fission debris radiation will affect the agent depends on the details of how the agent-filled containers are broken open by the blast and other explosion effects, and on the details of the subsequent dispersal of the spilled agent and its mixing with the rising fireball and fission debris cloud. All this is very difficult to treat in sufficient detail with available computer codes. On the other hand, the radiation dose deposited in the agent can be accurately computed given a particular storage configuration. This makes agent neutralization by the prompt radiation output a potentially attractive kill mechanism of nuclear warheads."

Kruger continued, "MCNP Monte Carlo radiation transport computations were performed exploring the capability of low-yield nuclear fusion and fission warheads to neutralize biological warfare agents with the radiation dose deposited in the agent by the prompt neutron output. The calculations were done for various typical storage configurations on the ground in the open air or in a warehouse building. This application of nuclear weapons is motivated by the observation that, for some military scenarios, the nuclear collateral effects area is much smaller than the area covered with unacceptable concentrations of biological agent dispersed by the use of conventional high explosive warheads.

"These calculations show that biological agents can be radiation-neutralized by low-yield nuclear warheads over areas that are sufficiently large to be useful for military strikes. This report provides the calculated doses within the stored agent for various ground ranges and heights-of-burst."

If the lethal agent was not biological, it may well have been chemical. UFO crash retrieval expert B.J. Booth believes that the Coyame deaths may have been caused by exposure to chemicals leaking from the crashed object. "I think it's most likely that some chemical agent used in the advanced systems of the UFO felled the

Mexicans."

Booth cites two other UFO crash retrievals in which UFO crashes led to health problems for those exposed to the area of the crash, "There is a report from Russia of a crashed disk recovery in 1991 in Shaitan Mazar. This case was reported by Emil Bachurin and Nikolay Subbotin. A recovery team reached the crash site and saw the elongated object crashed on the mountains. They were only able to approach the object to within a thousand feet or so. All of the team members were sickened, light headed, and disorientated. This may have been radiation, but it could have been some type of biological agent also. Also remember in the Rendlesham event of 1980, there were atmospheric anomalies present that caused the soldiers to be disorientated. This may have been lack of gravity, radiation, or some other agent."

Clearly, the events of the Coyame crash led U.S. military officials to believe that some form of deadly agent had been loosed upon the world. Their response was to explode crash debris and bodies that were suspected of having been contaminated. Although in retrospect, the action seems unprecedented in the annuals of international relations, it may have been motivated by an extreme fear of a catastrophic, worldwide epidemic of an extraterrestrial virus.

21. Nine Months After Coyame

The story of an airplane colliding with a UFO seems a highly unlikely scenario were it not for another terrifying event that occurred in the skies near Mexico City less than nine months after the Coyame incident. A Mexican pilot reported that on May 3, 1975, a UFO impacted the underside of his small plane in a harrowing episode during which three separate UFOs pursued him. Radar controllers later confirmed that they saw mysterious blips on radar, and the occupants of a passing plane also witnessed the event.

According to an account first published in the August 1975 bulletin of the Aerial Phenomena Research Organization, Inc. (APRO), the incident was reported by a 23-year-old Mexican citizen named Carlos Antonio De los Santos Montiel, the pilot and lone occupant of a Piper Aztec PA-24 airplane at the time of the event. The co-author of this book, UFO investigator Ruben Uriarte, who has researched the incident extensively and interviewed the pilot, said, "It's a very interesting story, and I have an audible tape of him screaming, 'Mayday, Mayday' to the air traffic controllers at the Mexico City airport. It was a very frightful event."

De los Santos Explains His Encounter (Courtesy of Ruben Uribe)

De los Santos' strange experience began with a routine flight from Mexico City to Lazaro Cardenas, a port city of Michoacan, located on Mexico's Pacific Coast. An employee of a Mexican company called Pelletier, S.A., De los Santos was assigned the task of transporting company personnel to Lazaro Cardenas. "The flight was from Mexico City to take company personnel to an iron and steel plant in Lazaro Cardenas," De los Santos later said.

After arriving safely and unloading his passengers at the Lazaro Cardenas Airport, De los Santos prepared for an immediate return to Mexico City, as per the instructions he had received from his employer. When he attempted to start his plane, however, he found that it would not start. After about a two-hour search for a mechanic, he found one, brought him to the airport, and managed to get the aircraft started.

Deciding that it was too late in the day to make the long flight back to Mexico City, De los Santos instead flew to nearby Zihuatanejo, Guerrero, a distance of about forty miles. In Zihuatanejo, he parked his aircraft, found a hotel, ate dinner, and retired early in order to prepare for an early departure the next morning.

On the following day, De los Santos woke up early, had a bath, and ate breakfast, before returning to the airfield for his departure. At about 10:30 a.m., he boarded his plane and took of off from Zihuatanejo, headed for Mexico City, some 200 air miles away. It was a cloudy and misty morning, with traces of smog in the air.

Arrow Shows Approximate Flight Path of De los Santos' Plane (Map Courtesy of U.T. Austin Libraries)

De los Santos climbed to approximately 15,000 feet in order to clear the poor visibility. Near midday, he was over Lake Tequesquitengo in Morelos, about 55 miles south of Mexico City. Wanting visual confirmation of his position, De los Santos brought his plane down through the cloud cover. He then received the shock of his life.

He said, "I took magnetic course 004, when after three or four seconds I had the sensation that something was close to the left wing; something there was watching."

Feeling a strange vibration in the plane, he looked to his right, where he saw, pacing alongside, a dark gray disk with a dome on top. De los Santos said, "I saw a dark gray colored object, rat gray, oval shaped, yes, with a type of control cockpit in the upper part, as a glass windshield, but dark. The inside of the object was not visible."

A second disk appeared to the left of the plane, causing the Mexican pilot an overwhelming sense of foreboding. "When seeing this one, I began to feel very nervous, even cried. It was like having a strange dream or hallucinations becoming real," he said.

A third disk approached head-on, before it dropped below the plane. De los Santos felt a jolt as if the object had dealt the plane a glancing blow along its bottom section.

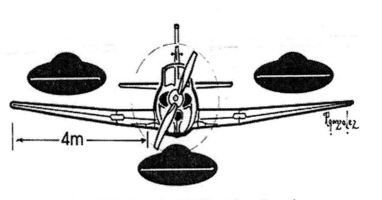

August 1975 Sketch by APRO's Robert Gonzalez

In the APRO account, De los Santos described the UFOs as having "the appearance of two plates joined together at the rim with a cupola which had what seemed to be a little window and an antenna on top." Regarding the disk that first approached head-on and then dipped down below, he later told investigators, "I was petrified after I saw a third object which seemed about to collide head-on with the windshield. But it went beneath the aircraft, and I heard a strange noise from below as though it had collided with the underside of the plane."

De los Santos later estimated that the flying dome-shaped discs were between 9 and 13 feet (3-4 meters) in diameter. The UFO that struck the aircraft over Coyame was said to be about 16 feet in diameter and also dome-shaped. In both incidents, the strange airships were small by UFO standards, leading some investigators to believe that they might have been pilot-less drones dispatched from a larger mother ship.

Referring to the De los Santos case, Ruben Uriarte said, "The saucers were roughly the same dimensions as the crashed saucer in Coyame. The saucers were escorting him on each side of his plane. There was another saucer underneath his fuselage."

When De los Santos tried to evade the UFOs by banking to his left, the horrified Mexican pilot realized that none of the controls of his plane would respond. An attempt to deploy his landing gear also failed.

Frantic, the pilot radioed to the air traffic controllers at the nearby Mexico City International Airport, "I am flying from Zihuatanejo, checked Tequesquitengo at 3,000 meters (10,000 feet), and have three visible objects flying around the aircraft. One is located on the right wing, another on the left wing, and the third under the aircraft. The third one came straight toward the aircraft from the front, ignoring the working propeller, and later hitting the underneath of the fuselage, next to the landing wheels, staying attached to that place. The other two are flying in a suspended position, not attached to the wings."

De los Santos continued, "My aircraft is out of control. I have no control over it. I have three unidentified objects flying around me. I have three unidentified flying objects flying around me; one came under my aircraft and hit it. The landing gear is locked in and the controls won't release them. My position – I am on the Radial 004 from the VOR Tequesquitengo. I am not controlling the plane. Control Mexico, can you hear me?" The time of De los Santos' distress call was logged as 12:15 p.m.

As the flying discs hovered around him, they exercised complete control of his plane. In addition to neutralizing all the aircraft's systems, the UFOs caught the plane in a sort of "tractor beam" and dragged it upward from an initial altitude of 3,000 meters (10,000 feet) to 4,500 meters (14,800 feet). The stunned pilot could only watch helplessly. He said, "This aircraft cannot fly above 4,500 meters because it does not have a pressurized cockpit."

Nearby, a Learjet aircraft registered as XC-SAG and in use by an agency of the Mexican government made visual contact with De los Santos' plane and the three mysterious objects hovering around it. The pilot of the Learjet radioed back to the Mexico City tower to confirm what he had seen.

This incredible air drama unfolded practically in the shadow of Mexico's famous twin volcanoes, Popocatépetl and Iztaccihuatl, whose shadowy forms loomed in the distance to the east of the Piper's position at the time of the encounter. Located about 40 miles southeast of Mexico City, the twin volcanoes have long been shrouded in legend and mystery.

Popocatepétl, which remains the most active volcano in North America, is a snow-capped peak that rises 13,776 ft above the surrounding basin. Mexico's ancient Aztec Indians gave the volcano its name, which means "Smoking Mountain". The area around Popocatépetl and Iztaccihuatl has long been associated with strange tales, including many UFO sightings, especially in the immediate vicinity of Popocatépetl. Striking photographs of flying discs hovering near the lofty volcano have been taken in recent years.

Because the area is constantly monitored by cameras due to its intense volcanic activity, many verifiable sightings have occurred. Most notable was a snapshot taken on June 29, 1999 by a surveillance camera of Mexico's disaster prevention agency, CENAPRED. At 1:20 p.m., the time-activated camera photographed a strange dark flying disk hovering near the volcano's crater, emerging from thick clouds of smoke. CENAPRED offered no explanation as to what the object may have been.

According to the Web site *UFOInfo*, "Mount Popocatépetl is probably Mexico's hottest UFO spot, with hundreds of sightings since 1993. Silver daylight discs have been seen and videotaped just west of the volcano at San Rafael, Ozumba, Tepetlixpa and Tlalmanalco, as well."

On May 3, 1974, these twin volcanoes stood as mute spectators to the amazing incident involving Carlos De los Santos Montiel. As the scared pilot watched, the UFO floating above his left wing suddenly moved. "The object on the left side rose vertically, and the rooftop of the aircraft prevent me from looking at this action, but then it flew towards Popocatépetl volcano, seeing this from the other window."

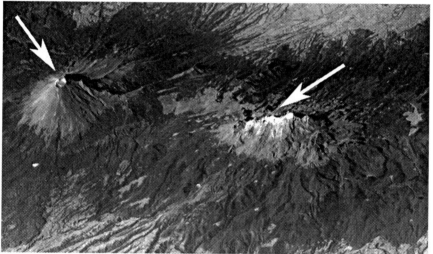

Mexico's Twin Volcanoes, Popocatépetl and Iztaccihuatl (NASA Photo)

"The object on the right side did not rise vertically up," De los Santos added, "Its motion was horizontal and following the object on the left side. I did not see again the one under the aircraft, but it must have followed the other two."

The objects, flying as one in a tight formation, sped off to the east toward Popocatépetl and Iztaccihuatl. De los Santos estimated their speed at about 900 kilometers per hour (1,448 miles per hour). As the UFOs disappeared out of view, the aircraft's systems suddenly returned to normal, and De los Santos regained control over his plane.

The shaken pilot proceeded to Mexico City International Airport, flying as fast as his small plane could go. "I was very nervous and began to speed up the aircraft to get as soon as possible to the Mexico City airport," De los Santos recalled.

Arriving over Mexico City, De los Santos discovered a problem with his landing gear. He told the control tower, "I have a problem with the landing wheels, have three green lights, but also have a false indication aboard. Could you check for the three wheels with binoculars?"

After flying near the control tower, De los Santos was informed that two of his wheels were only partly deployed and that the third wheel had not lowered at all. He continued circling for over an hour while attempting to lower all wheels. He said, "Being used to carrying some tools with me aboard, I took out a screwdriver, removed a register, and saw that a worm gear runs in there.... I introduced the screwdriver backwards to the motions of the worm gear, lowered the wheels, and it snapped free; so I knew it was down."

De Los Santos Headline in Mexico City Newspaper, May 5, 1975

At 1:34 p.m., De los Santos' nightmare finally ended, as he made an emergency landing, coming to rest in a grassy area between two runways. Fire trucks and an ambulance stood by as the plane's flight ended. "I did not turn off the engine, opened the door, jumped out of the aircraft, and began to run. An ambulance with a firefighter caught up with me and tried to calm me down. They helped me aboard the ambulance, where they gave me some tranquilizers."

De los Santos was transported to an airport clinic, where he received a medical exam and was found to be unharmed. The exam also ruled out that he was under the influence of drugs or alcohol. Although a doctor later theorized that low blood sugar might have caused De los Santos to hallucinate, there was no evidence to support that view.

After the incident, Emilio Estañol Lopez and Interian Diaz, air traffic controllers at Mexico City International Airport, told reporters that radar had painted another target in the vicinity of De los Santos' plane at the time of the incident. According to Estañol Lopez, the strange radar blip executed a 270-degree turn in a radius of 3 or 4 miles at a speed of about 575 miles per hour. Diaz stated that he knew of no manmade aircraft in 1975 that could execute such a maneuver.

The De los Santos Montiel incident, within the context of the crash near Coyame less than nine months later, remains of tremendous interest to UFO enthusiasts. "I believe there may be a connection with [this] experience several months earlier and the crash at Coyame," says Ruben Uriarte. The most compelling case for a relationship between these two cases is the virtually identical descriptions of the UFOs involved, as well as the fact that both involved a mid-air crash.

22. MEXICO'S 1977 UFO CRASH

As if the 1974 Coyame incident were not incredible enough, at least one other significant UFO crash retrieval event was reported in Mexico in the 1970s. The incident first came to light in an article titled "UFO Travelers Searched For" in the September 5, 1977 edition of *Cronica*, a newspaper in Buenos Aires, Argentina. The Argentineans claimed to have obtained the story from a Mexican newspaper identified as *La Prensa*, which may have been Mexico City's daily newspaper of the same name.

"Mexican soldiers are looking for some little men with square feet and luminous suits who dropped from the sky about a month ago," *Cronica* reported. According to the article, two UFO occupants died at the scene, but "several of the crew escaped alive."

The exact location of the crash is not given, as the article mentions only that it occurred somewhere in "the Sierra Madre Mountains." Since there are four mountain ranges in Mexico referred to as "Sierra Madre," this description is not helpful in determining the crash site. The Sierra Madre Occidental parallels Mexico's Pacific Coast and is an extension of California's Sierra Nevada. The Sierra Madre Oriental extends from the U.S. Rocky Mountains south, paralleling Mexico's Gulf Coast. The Sierra Madre del Sur and the Sierra Madre de Chiapas are located in the country's southernmost region.

Following the UFO crash, which was said to have occurred in August of 1977, at least 200 Mexican soldiers were dispatched to the area in an effort to secure the crash site and recover both the living and dead alien beings. "A brief report states that at least 200 Mexican soldiers were searching for little men with square feet and luminous suits who dropped from the sky about a month ago," says the *UFOinfo* Web site. "Newspaper reports stated that a saucer had crashed … and that there had been several survivors among its occupants. Police were also reportedly at the scene of the crash. No other information."

This reported UFO crash may be related to several other incidents reported in July and August of 1977 in the southern part of

Mexico. In "UFO Crashes in Latin America," Scott Corrales states, "In July 1977, hundreds of awed witnesses were able to behold a number of falling unidentified flying objects, some of which were even captured on film. The mobilization of the Mexican Army over the course of the following days made many realize that something significant had indeed transpired, and rumors spread about a UFO which had collided in the mountains."

Physiographic Map of Mexico Showing Mountain Ranges (Map Courtesy of U.T. Austin Libraries)

Corrales continues, "The town of Jopala, to the east of Puebla and in the vicinity of the Gulf of Mexico, became the target of serious research. The townspeople had allegedly seen a solid craft explode into thousands of sparks: witnesses included not only the local mayor, but also a number of schoolteachers, who had been able to retrieve pieces of a rough metal."

"The most curious detail to the townspeople's story was that others had beaten them to recover the pieces of the unusual material -- a group of persons who arrived by helicopter and were obviously Americans. The news media would later report, as it often does, that 'NASA scientists' had visited the area...

133

"Upon analysis, one of the recovered pieces of UFO debris proved to be an unusually pure alloy, unavailable to earthly technology at the time. U.S. researchers also believed that a subsequent collision had occurred in Tabasco, and that two dead alien pilots had been recovered from the wreckage. Mexican researchers were greatly annoyed at the fact that foreign investigators had obtained access to the available data before their own research teams."

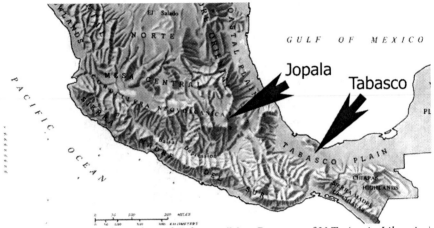

Relative Positions of Jopala and Tabasco (Map Courtesy of U.T. Austin Libraries)

It is possible that the *Cronica* newspaper account and the events described by Corrales are actually all related. Perhaps the UFO explosion that caused debris to rain down in Jopala (near the Sierra Madre Oriental) was followed by the crash of the same object in the Sierra Madre Mountains near Tabasco state. It seems conceivable that this occurrence was the basis of the September 5, 1977 article in *Cronica*.

Regardless of whether the three events are related or not, we can be certain that some very unusual UFO events occurred over Mexico in July and August of 1977, culminating in either one or possibly two separate UFO crashes. These incidents help to further amplify the significance of the Coyame event in 1974, and they also underscore the key role that Mexico has played in the history of UFO crash retrievals.

23. THE NOBEL LAUREATE

Some UFO researchers believe that Hispanic physicist Luis W. Alvarez, who was of Spanish descent, may have assisted the U.S. government with the investigation of one or more UFO crash retrievals in Northern Mexico over the course of his long career. Alvarez, a Nobel-prize winning physicist, was one of America's foremost scientists from the 1940s through the 1980s. During his wide-ranging career, he invented key wartime radar systems for the U.S. military, helped birth the atomic bomb, and developed a liquid-hydrogen bubble chamber that allowed close study of atomic particles. What is particularly intriguing about Alvarez, however, is that, in addition to his work in physics, he had a passion for exploring the hidden mysteries of the universe, as is evident from the fact that he used his scientific know-how to delve into UFOs, the Egyptian pyramids, the John F. Kennedy assassination, and the extinction of the dinosaurs.

Dr. Luis W. Alvarez (U.S. Government Photo)

In the late 1970s, Alvarez stunned scientists throughout the world by advancing the theory that dinosaurs were wiped out when either comets or asteroids collided with the earth, thus changing the planet's atmosphere. Although the theory was initially criticized and even ridiculed by some, it has since gained widespread acceptance.

Following Alvarez's death in 1988, a colleague told the Associated Press, "Luis Alvarez was a stunningly creative individual. His discoveries and inventions spanned an amazing range of the frontiers of man's knowledge over more than half a century."

Alvarez's military contract work early in his career led to him becoming a staunch supporter and defender of the U.S. military and its initiatives over the years. Consequently, the U.S. government often used Alvarez as a consultant on special projects, such as the Central Intelligence Agency's *Scientific Advisory Panel on Unidentified Flying Objects*, also known as the "Robertson Panel," of 1953.

During their deliberations, Alvarez and the other Panel members looked at several specific UFO cases from the 1940s and 1950s (pre-selected by the CIA), none of which seemed overly impressive to them. The Panel upheld the standard CIA position that the specific UFO cases they looked at had normal, rational explanations based on scientific fact. The Panel's reports state "none of the members of the Panel were loath to accept that this earth might be visited by extraterrestrial intelligent beings of some sort, some day." Their negative finding was based merely on the few specific UFO cases that the Panel examined in 1953.

But the most significant thing about the Robertson Panel is its strong recommendation that the U.S. government engage in "debunking" UFO stories in order to prevent Russia from somehow using the American public's strong interest in UFOs for propaganda purposes. The Panel recommended the strategy of immediately countering stories about UFO sightings with scientific analysis designed to remove the allure of the unknown. The Panel concluded, "As in the case of conjuring tricks, there is much less stimulation if the 'secret' is known. Such a [debunking] program should tend to reduce the current gullibility of the public and consequently their susceptibility to clever hostile propaganda." The Panel reiterated its fear that the UFO phenomenon provided the Soviet Union with "so many obvious possibilities for exploitation."

The Robertson Panel further recommended the use of the national media to "debunk" UFO stories. Disney cartoons were cited as a clever way to attack the credibility of UFO sightings. The Panel also suggested employing the services of psychologists "familiar with mass psychology" and amateur astronomers.

Clearly, Cold War tensions were a major motivator for the U.S. government's desire to keep UFO secrets in the late 1940s and early 1950s. It is also clear that, despite official claims that the Panel's recommendations were never actually implemented, its debunking policy eventually became deeply engrained in the culture of how the U.S. government dealt with UFO sightings. The entire document with the conclusions and recommendations of the Robertson Panel is available as an appendix to this book.

In the years following the Robertson Panel's work, the name of Panel Member Luis W. Alvarez became linked with the supposed crash retrieval of a UFO in the Sierra Madre Oriental Mountains of northeastern Mexico in the late 1940s.

Arrow Shows Approximate Impact Point of Laredo 1948 UFO Crash (Map Courtesy of U.T. Austin Libraries)

The reported UFO crash site, about 25 miles west-southwest of Zapata, Texas, is located in the foothills that comprise the beginning of the Sierra Madre Oriental mountain range. Steinman and Stevens state, "This site was about 30 miles SSW of Laredo, not far from the highway to Mexico City, and near where the Rio Sabinas joins the Rio Salado before they empty into the Rio Grande, in the Sierra Madre Oriental. Is this the site in the Sierra Madre mountains of Nuevo Leon where Dr. [Luis] W. Alvarez, a physicist from the University of California in Los Angeles, together with other scientists, was taken in July of 1948 to examine the residue on site of a crashed 100 foot diameter circular flying vehicle of unknown origin?"

Although it is unknown whether Alvarez was involved in the Coyame crash of 1974, he could have been, given his sterling scientific credentials, his high military clearance, his strong interest in the paranormal, and his familiarity with Mexico.

24. U.S.-MEXICO UFO RELATIONS

The Coyame crash of 1974 was certainly not the first time that the topic of unidentified flying saucers had arisen in the arena of U.S.-Mexico international relations. Since both governments maintain official silence regarding any agreements or policies toward UFOs, only rarely has the public caught a glimpse of the hidden "UFO relations" between the two countries. One such glimpse is possible in a remarkable series of events involving a former Mexican president.

Miguel Alemán Valdez served as Mexico's president from 1946 to 1952. His term in office corresponded with that of Harry S. Truman, who was the U.S. President from 1945 to 1953. When Miguel Alemán and Truman held talks in Mexico City during March 3-5, 1947, it was the first time an American President officially visited the Mexican capital. The visit was a friendly one, and discussions were held on several topics, including U.S. loans to foreign countries and outbreaks of a disease affecting livestock in both countries. Some researchers think that the topic of UFOs may also have come up between the two men when meeting in private.

Miguel Alemán (left) meets with Harry S. Truman in 1947 (Truman Presidential Library)

139

Speaking in Mexico's National Palace on March 3, in a nationwide radio broadcast, Truman said, "International relations have traditionally been compared to a chess game in which each nation tries to outwit and checkmate the other. I cannot accept that comparison with respect to the relations between your country and mine, Mr. President [Miguel Alemán]. The United States and Mexico are working together for the mutual benefit of their peoples and the peace of the world. You have made me feel, what I could not have doubted in any case, that I stand here, in the midst of the great people of Mexico, as a trusted friend and a welcome guest."

Truman's historic visit to Mexico City in March was followed by a reciprocal visit by Miguel Alemán to Washington, DC two months later, from April 29 to May 1. This was the first time a Mexican President officially visited the United States capital. On May 1, he delivered a historic address in a joint meeting of the U.S. Congress.

Mexican Army Units in Mexico City Parade (U.S. Air Force Photo)

In the *Library of Congress Country Studies*, the Alemán presidency is described as follows: "One of Alemán's first acts as president was to reaffirm amicable postwar relations between Mexico and the United States. In a symbolic gesture of rapprochement, United States President Harry S. Truman and President Alemán visited each other's countries. On September 2, 1947, Mexico was among the signatories of the Inter-American Treaty of Reciprocal Assistance (Rio Treaty), which outlined a system of mutual defense on the part of Western Hemisphere nations against outside aggression."

It is extremely interesting to UFO researchers that three important Mexican crash retrieval events (Laredo 1948, Mexico City 1949, and Del Rio 1950) all occurred during this era of improved relations between Mexico and the United States. In all three crashes, the administration of Miguel Alemán Valdez seems to have cooperated with the Truman White House.

In the 1948 crash near Laredo, Mexican troops stood down, allowing the Americans full access to the crash site. In the 1950 crash near Del Rio, the Mexican soldiers reportedly secured the area of the crash, waited for the U.S. troops to arrive, and then turned the crash scene over to the Americans. In the 1949 crash near Mexico City, the Mexicans were said to have allowed a number of U.S. military officials to visit the crash site.

In yet another interesting fact about the relationship between Miguel Alemán and Harry S. Truman, both men were members of the Freemasons in their respective countries. Truman even rose to the rank of Grand Master.

Although Miguel Alemán had already left Mexico's highest political office by the time Dwight Eisenhower became U.S. president in 1953, he communicated with Eisenhower on occasion, including at a "summit of ex-presidents" held in January of 1963.

In 1982, Leonard Stringfield reported that former Mexican president Miguel Alemán claimed that Eisenhower once told him an amazing story about UFOs. Eisenhower claimed he had visited an air base in the Southwestern United States where he was shown a recovered flying saucer and its dead crew.

In his *UFO Crash/Retrieval Status Report III*, Stringfield revealed a letter written by a UFO researcher from Madrid, Spain named Antonio Ribera. According to Ribera, a friend of his attended a gathering in Mexico in 1970 at which one of the guests was former Mexican President Miguel Alemán Valdez. The evening's conversation turned to the subject of unidentified flying objects, which caused the former president to listen attentively but say nothing. When one of the guests noticed that Miguel Alemán had not given his opinion, he asked the former president what he thought about flying saucers.

Alemán's response most certainly shocked everyone at the table that evening, as he revealed that during a meeting with Dwight D. Eisenhower, the former U.S. President had told Alemán that he had once been taken to a military base and shown a crashed flying saucer and its dead occupants.

In his letter to Stringfield, Ribera stated, "Eisenhower told him [Alemán] that he once visited an air base in the Southwest United States where they showed him a flying disk and the cadavers of several of its crew members."

Harry S. Truman (left) and General Dwight D. Eisenhower (right). (Eisenhower Presidential Library)

Skeptics argue that Eisenhower was not the U.S. President when Miguel Alemán was in office; however, the meeting between

Alemán and Eisenhower may have taken place after Alemán left office. Former presidents in Mexico continue to use the title of president even after their term ends, as is also the practice in the United States. The Alemán-Eisenhower meeting might even have taken place in January 1963 when the two former presidents met in Washington, D.C. for a series of talks.

Regardless of when the meeting took place, the story that Eisenhower supposedly told Alemán about having seen a crashed UFO and its occupants is incredible indeed. Given that the Alemán presidency was a time of great UFO activity in both Mexico and the United States, this remains an intriguing story.

25. THE MEXICAN MISSILE CRISIS

Skeptics have suggested that the Coyame UFO crash retrieval story may be nothing more than folklore arising from incidents where U.S. military missiles went astray and crashed into Northern Mexico. While it is true that there have been three or four accidental missile crashes in Mexico, the authors do not believe that these stray missiles are sufficient to explain away the UFO crash retrieval evidence that forms the basis of this book. However, because the missile events do serve to shed light on the UFO stories, we will fully explore the documentary evidence behind the known cases of U.S. missiles crashing in Northern Mexico.

The missile cases yield valuable insight into how the U.S. and Mexico have dealt with crash retrieval scenarios. Like the UFO events, the missile crashes brought the two governments into diplomatic dialogue regarding the recovery of the crashed objects. During suspected UFO crash retrievals, the U.S. has been accused of claiming to be engaged in recovering a fallen missile or experimental aircraft in order to hide the truth about crashed UFOs.

Werner Von Braun Holds a V-2 Model, Circa 1950 (NASA Photo)

144

The first confirmed crash of a U.S. missile in Mexico occurred during the very early days of U.S. rocket research. In the mid 1940s, thousands of V-2 rocket parts taken from the Germans after World War II were shipped to Fort Bliss, Texas and White Sands, New Mexico, where they were used to build America's early missile arsenal. A team of captured German rocket scientists, including future NASA wizard Werner Von Braun, worked at a makeshift Fort Bliss camp to recreate and expand the rocket work they had done for Adolf Hitler.

On May 29, 1947 at 8:30 p.m., Von Braun's team launched one of their 46-foot tall rockets from a White Sands firing site at Tularosa Basin, located 44 miles north of El Paso, Texas. The rocket was supposed to fly north for 40 miles and then come down still within the White Sands compound. Instead, after a gyroscope failure, the missile spun around almost 180 degrees and veered south into Mexico. The *New York Times* reported, "It soared into the night sky, but instead of arching northward into the desert, it backtracked, roared southward over El Paso and fell with a loud explosion somewhere south of the Rio Grande."

V-2 Rocket Launch From White Sands (U.S. Air Force Photo)

The rocket, which was the twenty-eighth V-2 test missile to be launched in the U.S., was traveling at more than 1,000 miles per hour when it slammed into the ground just south of Ciudad Juarez, Chihuahua, near the Tepeyac Cemetery. The U.S. Army later identified the V-2 as "Missile 0 of the Hermes series."

According to the *Chicago Daily Tribune*, the resulting explosion and rising column of smoke led many residents of the area to believe that an Atomic bomb had landed nearby. The 200,000 residents of El Paso-Juarez were so shaken that many of them made panicked phone calls to their local police and media, causing telephone circuits to become hopelessly jammed. "Women knelt praying in the streets, excited motorists smashed autos, and many persons believed an atom bomb had hit," said the newspaper.

"Juarez eyewitnesses reported 'a blinding flash of light' followed by a tremendous pressure wave, followed by the appearance of a mushroom cloud," according to an account in J. Andrew Kissner's *Peculiar Phenomenon: Early United States Efforts to Collect and Analyze Flying Discs.* "The mushroom cloud excited local rumors that an atomic bomb had exploded. The concussion of the blast was sufficient to crack windows six miles north of the crash site, while an electric clock stopped, apparently due to some blast effect at the El Paso County Sheriff's Office. The ground shock generated by the explosion was felt 35 miles northwest of the impact crater."

"Lt. Colonel Harold R. Turner, White Sands commandant, said the modified V-2 rocket, fired at 8:30 p.m. had deviated from its set northerly course because of a failure in its German-made gyroscope. The explosion occurred about three minutes later," the *Chicago Daily Tribune* said. Mexican officials in Juarez reported no casualties and no property damage.

The *Los Angeles Times* quoted Harold R. Turner as saying that a gyroscope that should have controlled the V-2 on its 40-mile flight from one end of the range to the other somehow became reversed. Instead of heading north, the V-2 shot off to the south. A civilian technician at White Sands misread data and failed to hit the abort switch that would have remotely cut off the rocket's fuel and would have brought it down in the desert within 25 miles of the launch point.

Turner told the newspaper, "It's a miracle no one was killed or even injured. If the missile had impacted in a residential area in Juarez, it could have been a major disaster."

On the morning after the crash, even as U.S. diplomats in

Mexico City delivered an apology, hundreds of Mexicans and Texans gathered around what the *New York Times* described as "the great crater that was scooped out by the rocket in the rocky knob of a little mesa near a cemetery and the Juarez airfield, about three to four miles from the Juarez-El Paso bridges."

Newspaper reports indicated that U.S. military recovery teams headed to Juarez by air and by ground immediately after the crash. Kissner says, "MPs stationed at Ft. Bliss and other U.S. Army personnel from WSPG [White Sands Proving Grounds] rushed across the border into Mexico in an attempt to secure the downed object. They were met at the crater by Mexican troops and summarily evicted. Mexico's General Enrique Diaz Gonzalez commanded the Juarez Garrison. Gen Gonzalez placed Juarez off limits to U.S. Army personnel for several weeks after the explosion."

According to Kissner, the crashed missile was totally vaporized, leaving only small shreds of "burned gray metal fused with molten sand and rock" around the 50' x 50' x 24' crater. The Mexican military's recovery efforts yielded only enough debris to fit comfortably on top of a single desk.

The Second Crash

A second V-2 crash reportedly occurred five months later in nearly the same spot, although the U.S. military never admitted that the second object was one of theirs. The mystery missile fell from the sky on October 12, 1947, landing in a hilly area near Guadalupe, Chihuahua, Mexico, about ten miles from the site of the May 29 incident.

"An unidentified flaming object soared over the Texas-Mexico border today, apparently smashing into the Samalayuca Mountains of Mexico with a loud explosion and billows of smoke," the Associated Press reported. "The approximate imact area was estimated to be less than 10 miles from The point where a V-2 rocket, off its track, crashed south of Juarez May 29. At least four persons saw the fiery object darting through the skies 'with the speed of a falling star' at approximately 9:30 a.m."

An eyewitness told the *Chicago Daily Tribune* that he was

standing at a filling station in Guadalupe at about 9:30 a.m. when he observed a brilliant light about 100 feet up in the sky moving rapidly from east to west and trailing a blue flame. The witness, a retired Mexican army officer, said the object "looked like a meteor."

The object impacted the earth with a booming noise and a towering plume of smoke. The impact site was at a point across the Rio Grande River from Fabens, Texas. A recently declassified Army report described the UFO as "a mysterious object which blazed through the sky, crashed and apparently exploded in the mountains near the village of Caseta, Mexico, across the Rio Grande from Fabens, Texas."

The Associated Press said, "It was reported to have come from the direction of the United States, and it produced a sizeable crater on impact. Members of the Mexican Army who visited the site stated that the object was another V-2 similar to the May 29 incident, and the Mexican War Department issued a statement repeating the claim." The U.S. Army's report on the matter added, "The War Department in Mexico City asserted … that investigation indicated the object was a V-2 rocket launched from a U.S. Army experimental station in Texas."

> The following message received from Gen Homer commanding Ft Bliss Texas via telephone 2400Z hours is quoted: "This is a report of a minor and unusual incident not of national interest. It is alleged that as of 1530Z an aerial object landed in Mexico near the towns of Cassetta-Reforma - Guadeloupe all opposite Fabens Texas. Object approximately one meter long traveling east to west, blue or silver in color with flames in the rear. No smoke, object alleged to have detonated with explosion beyond horizon in Mexico. I, Gen Homer have made recon of area and have interviewed available witnesses. American consul has transmitted the foregoing to American Embassy in Mexico. There are no military activities at Biggs Field, White Sands Proving Grounds, or Ft Bliss that could have caused this incident on this date. Army Ground Forces will be notified by me. The press and radio locally and New York Times representative from Los Angeles now checking the incident. No action required by higher headquarters. Available information at this time is not adequate to estimate cause of the indicent. End." Additional information when and if available will be forwarded.

Excerpt From U.S. Army Report 10-13-47 (Project Blue Book)

U.S. military officials, however, claimed that no U.S. rockets or aircraft of any kind were responsible for the Guadalupe crash. According to an AP report, a spokesman for the White Sands Missile Range said no missiles had been launched from there since October 9. "Major General John L. Homer, Fort Bliss commander and military officials at air fields and other installations in the Southwest, said that no guided missiles had been fired today and no rocket planes were missing from the fields in the area."

The crash site itself failed to yield any debris or clues of any kind other than the impact crater. The U.S. military reiterated that none of its installations had launched any sort of rocket or missile on October 12.

In a recently declassified memo from the U.S. National Archives, the U.S. military attaché in Mexico City wrote the following on October 16, 1947: "A mysterious object which fell near Guadalupe, Chihuahua (48 km Southeast of El Paso) on 12 October has been the source of much speculation in the press. According to a sergeant of the 35th Infantry Battalion who visited the crater and reported to the 5th Zone Commander, the object was a V-2. With this as a basis, Defense Nacional announced officially that it was a V-2 similar to the one which fell near Ciudad Juarez on 29 May 1947. General Homer, commanding Fort Bliss, has categorically stated that no V-2 was fired on that date. A-1 comment: It is believed that the Mexican Army source is incompetent to make a declaration as to whether it was or was not a V-2 but an official U.S. Government announcement seems required at this time, as sovereignty of Mexican soil in involved."

Days later, apparently after high level negotiations between the two governments, Mexican officials began backing off from their earlier statements that the crashed object was another V-2 rocket. The concept that it was a fallen meteorite suddenly gained favor.

An October 16 U.S. Army press release announced, "Gen. Enrique Diaz Gonzales, who commands the Juarez military garrison just across the border from El Paso, today blamed a 'false report' for the Mexican War Department's announcement that an American rocket landed south of here last Sunday."

20 Years Later

It was twenty years before another piece of U.S. military hardware was confirmed to have crashed in Mexico. In the first incident involving a missile designed to carry a nuclear payload, a medium-range Pershing ballistic missile spun out of control and crashed 200 miles south of the Texas-Mexico border in 1967.

Designed as a mobile missile, the Pershing featured two solid-fuel engine stages and an inertial guidance system. At the very top of the sharply tipped cone, the missile could carry up to a 400-kiloton nuclear warhead. The Pershing, which had a functional range of 460 miles, stood just over 34 feet tall and was slightly more than 3 feet in diameter.

On September 12, 1967, a Pershing I missile was launched from Blanding, Utah, on a heading that would cause it to crash on the grounds of the White Sands Missile Range in southern New Mexico. The missile's trajectory quickly deviated from what its planners had in mind.

Pershing Missile Launch (U.S. Army Photo)

The errant missile overshot its target in New Mexico, and crashed across the Rio Grande River, south of Van Horn, Texas, in the Mexican state of Chihuahua. The missile crashed approximately 250 miles farther south than intended, finally coming to rest in a remote stretch of Mexican desert, very close to the site of the reported 1974 Coyame UFO crash.

The *New York Times* reported, "A 10,000-pound Army Pershing missile fired from Utah went off course today and landed in Mexico. The Mexican Government gave the United States Government permission to send a helicopter across the Rio Grande to look for it."

"Officials at White Sands said that the supersonic, 35-foot-tall

Pershing was capable of carrying a nuclear warhead but carried only an unarmed dummy warhead on today's training flight. No property damage or injuries were reported."

The *New York Times* stated that earlier on the same day, West German Air Force troops had successfully launched a Pershing missile, which later crashed in White Sands, New Mexico. The cause of failure for the U.S. Army's missile was unknown.

Quoted in the same article, the sheriff of Culberson County, Texas, said that the missile had crashed "near El Cuervo, about 20 miles into Mexico, 45 miles from Van Horn."

A day later, the *New York Times* reported that the U.S. Army helicopter search team failed to find "any trace" of the Pershing missile. About a week later, though, a Mexican rancher found metal debris in an area 50 miles southwest of Van Horn, Texas. The U.S. government again requested permission from the Mexicans to "inspect the area and remove any components that may be found."

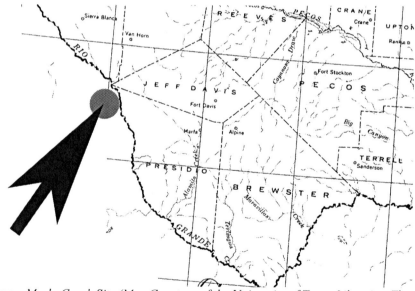

Arrow Marks Crash Site (Map Courtesy of the University of Texas Libraries, The University of Texas at Austin.)

After being granted permission, U.S. military officials, accompanied by Mexican ranchers, finally located and recovered "critical" components of the crashed missile from the Chihuahuan desert near El Cuervo. The drama of the fallen Pershing was ended.

The crash of the Pershing missile in Mexico created a bit of an international incident, as later admitted in a U.S. Army historical document by Jim Eckles. The U.S. government quickly mobilized its diplomatic corps to profusely apologize to the Mexicans and assure them that the event was merely an unavoidable accident.

Athena Missile Being Prepared for Launch (U.S. Air Force Photo)

Radioactive Missile Lands in Mexico

A much more serious diplomatic incident occurred three years later, when a U.S. missile carrying radioactive Cobalt 57 crashed in the desert near Ceballos, Durango, Mexico, about 200 miles south of the Texas border. It was after the crash of this missile that the desert around Ceballos gained notoriety as Mexico's "Zone of Silence."

The incident began with the firing of Athena missile number 122 on July 11, 1970 from an Air Force test facility in Green River, Utah. Standing 50 feet tall and weighing 16,000 pounds, the Athena was a scaled-down version of an intercontinental ballistic missile (ICBM). The Air Force used the Athena to study reentry characteristics of warheads and other space vehicles. Tests of full-scale ICBMs were only done at sea.

According to Jim Eckles' article "The Athena That Got Away," the missile's first two stages were designed to push the Athena to an altitude of about 200 miles. Once there, computers reoriented the missile so that it pointed down toward White Sands, New Mexico. At that point, stages three and four fired in sequence, hurling the reentry vehicle back to earth at speeds of up to 15,250 miles per hour.

The flight of Athena number 122 proceeded without a hitch until reentry. Due to the communications blackout that occurs when any spacecraft is reentering the earth's atmosphere, flight controllers at White Sands were unable to detect that a deviation in course had occurred.

According to Eckles, a White Sands technician peeked outside, looking for the telltale glow of the Athena coming into the atmosphere toward White Sands. The technician was shocked to see the rocket's glare almost directly overhead and still streaking to the south toward Texas.

Still uncertain where exactly the missile had gone, White Sands personnel spent time searching the missile range and reviewing telemetry before finally concluding that the Athena must have gone down somewhere in Mexico. The July 12 edition of the *Los Angeles Times* quoted White Sands officials that "the missile probably landed in mountains 180 miles southeast of Chihuahua City about 400 miles south of where it should have landed on the missile range." The article also noted that the Air Force was negotiating through diplomatic channels for permission to enter Mexico and search for the missile.

On July 13, Mexican federal troops, escorted by local ranchers, reportedly visited a debris field near Ceballos, Durango, where "chunks of metal were scattered across the desert." The U.S. Air

Force grew even more eager to visit the crash area. The *Washington Post* reported, "The Air Force had said it believed the Athena's instrument-laden nose cone survived the crash but search crews were delayed in crossing the border by diplomatic protocol." White Sands spokesman Jim Lovelady said that after the missile crash, the U.S. had to wait patiently for Mexican approval, due to an agreement between the two countries.

In 1992, Andrea Kaus, an anthropology student from California, summarized what happened next, "Hardly anyone saw the rocket fall. A few shepherds in the hills thought perhaps an angel had fallen. A rancher living close by was frightened and then angered as his cattle broke out of the corrals in their panic. People in the towns attributed the flash of light to an unusually bright falling star or meteorite. Maybe nothing more would have been said, except that the U.S. government came looking for its wayward missile and did not want anyone to know about it. Consistent with governmental common sense, no one asked the rancher whose cattle had been spooked where the missile had landed, or even asked anyone residing in the general vicinity. Instead, people from Gomez-Palacio were hired to scour (quietly) the Bolson for the missing missile while U.S. planes scouted from the air. It was finally found after three weeks, buried nose-first in a sand dune."

On July 16, a U.S. search team left White Sands headed for the reported crash site in Mexico. Eckles wrote, "By the time the group left on July 16, the data reduction folks deduced that the Athena was 450 miles into Mexico in a south-southeast direction in the area of the boundary between Durango and Chihuahua."

On the recovery team was White Sands project engineer Carlos Bustamante, who was chosen apparently because he spoke Spanish. The team leader was Lt. Colonel Lowell "Buzz" Knight. Part of the team flew down to Mexico in two small contracted airplanes, while other team members drove to the crash area in two vehicles that were also to be used for the retrieval operation. The members of the team established a base in Torreon, Coahuila, the largest town in the area of the crash.

The Americans met with a Mexican team consisting of army personnel and scientists. Two Mexican army officers spoke English, and thus Bustamante's services as a translator were no longer required.

The U.S. team began flying reconnaissance missions over the surrounding open desert and mountainous terrain, while other team members interviewed local residents about what they saw or heard on July 11. The search quickly became tedious and protracted.

On July 29, Mexican Foreign Relations Secretary Antonio Carillo Flores announced that he had received assurances from the U.S. State Department that the Americans would not be firing any more Athena missiles until the problems that caused the July 11 crash were found and corrected.

Carlos Bustamante (U.S. Air Force Photo)

The nose cone containing the radioactive Cobalt 57 was finally located on August 2 by a specially equipped aircraft on loan from the Atomic Energy Commission. An onboard scintillometer and spectrum analyzer allowed the crew to fix the exact position of the nose cone on the desert floor below. After the plane dropped sacks of flour to mark the way, the other members of the team, led by Bustamante, finally arrived at the nose cone debris.

The team found a small crater area with just a few pieces of twisted metal and some contaminated sand. The Cobalt 57 contained in the nose cone was a very small amount that was used for testing and was not meant to be a weapon. The recovery crew detected a very low level of radioactivity at the site.

Although the radioactivity was extremely low, negotiations

between the U.S. and Mexico resulted in an agreement for the Americans to remove most of the contaminated soil and to bury the rest. Thus, "Operation Sand Patch" was born, which by October 1, 1970, had removed sixty barrels of contaminated soil from the area.

On October 7, the radioactive soil arrived on the grounds of the White Sands Missile Range, marking the conclusion of Operation Sand Patch. The total cost of the recovery effort was $104,000.

The exact cause of the Athena's guidance failure was never determined. Athena testing resumed in January of 1971 and continued through the summer of 1973.

The Athena Mexico Cleanup (U.S. Air Force Photo)

Thus end the three known cases (and one suspected case) of U.S. military missiles crashing in Northern Mexico. While these missile crashes may seem to be a possible explanation for the stories of fallen UFOs in Northern Mexico, a careful examination of the facts demonstrates that this is not necessarily the case. The authors contend that tales of crashed missiles and experimental aircraft eventually became a convenient cover story for use when the U.S. military wanted to wrap a veil of secrecy over crashed objects that were truly unknown.

26. WATCHING THE BORDER

Four years after the reported UFO crash near Coyame, Chihuahua, the U.S. military quietly began putting into place a network of tethered observation blimps all along the Rio Grande River. These inflated static aircraft, called *aerostats*, are raised aloft and cabled in place, for use as radar stations along the U.S.-Mexico border. Operated by the Air Force and the U.S. Customs service, their stated mission is to detect aircraft entering into the country from the south. The system employs several unmanned Aerostats along the southern border of the United States, most notably in Marfa, Texas (near Coyame); Eagle Pass, Texas (near Del Rio); and Rio Grande City, Texas (south of Laredo). Interestingly, each aerostat floats almost exactly above reported locations of three major Texas-Mexico UFO crash retrievals: the 1974 Coyame case, the 1950 crash of a UFO near Del Rio, and the 1948 UFO crash near Laredo.

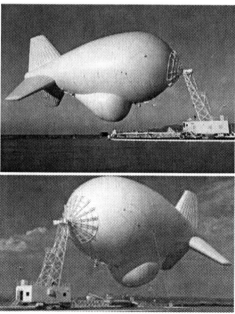

Tethered Aerostats (U.S. Government Photos)

Each aerostat, attached by a 25,000-foot cable, is about twice the size of the Goodyear blimp, carries two different kinds of radar systems, and has a maximum detection range of 200 miles. The U.S. Air Force fact sheet about these tethered aircraft states, "The radar data of the aerostat is available to NORAD Command and the U.S. Customs Service. In addition, this information is available to a blockhouse ground station below, where a flight controller, seated before banks of meters and television screens, monitors the balloon's performance. All radar data is transmitted to the ground station, then digitized and fed to the various control centers for display."

As of January 2003, the Air Force reported operational tethered aerostats at the following locations: Yuma and Fort Huachuca, Ariz.; Deming, N.M.; Marfa, Eagle Pass, and Rio Grande City, Texas; Cudjoe Key, Fla.; and Lajas, Puerto Rico.

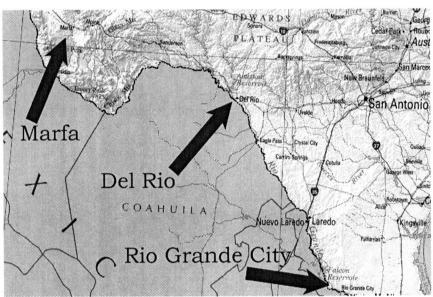

Map Showing Texas Aerostat Locations (UT-Austin Libraries)

Among the aerostat locations outside of Texas is Lajas, Puerto Rico, which has been known as a hotbed of UFO sightings and activities for many years. In a September 28, 2005 article for the Associated Press, Alexandra Olson wrote, "People in this sleepy hamlet are so sure they have been receiving other-worldly visitors, they want to build a UFO landing strip to welcome them. A bright green sign along a lonely country road in southwestern Puerto Rico proudly displays a silhouette of a flying saucer and two words: 'Extraterrestrial Route.'"

The article went on to report that the mayor of Lajas, Marcos Irizarry, is among the town's many residents who insist they have seen UFOs. "It's a very mysterious place," said Irizarry, who claims he once saw red lights zigzagging above the hills. "A lot of people have seen things."

The story concludes, "But it's a little-known aerostat off the Extraterrestrial Route that inspires UFO lore in Lajas. The U.S. military uses the aerostat, a tethered blimp with a radar system, to detect low-flying drug smuggling planes. But many Lajans don't believe that. Even Irizarry has suggested that the aerostat's true purpose is to detect UFOs."

The Puerto Rico Aerostat and Warning Sign (1994 by Ruben Uriarte)

During a 1994 expedition to Lajas, Puerto Rico, co-author Ruben Uriarte photographed the aerostat and a nearby sign that warns, "Notice. You are approaching restricted federal property. Use of deadly force is authorized in this area."

Is it coincidental that U.S. government tethered aerostat observation stations tend to show up in areas with documented UFO activity? Could the three aerostats along the Texas-Mexico border be keeping a wary eye out not just for drug traffickers, but also for strange aircraft darting in and out among the rugged mountain peaks of northern Mexico?

The Marfa, Texas, aerostat location is intriguing because of its proximity (90 miles) to Coyame, Chihuahua, and the fact that it overlooks one of the Lone Star State's oldest and most mysterious unexplained phenomenon, the Marfa Lights. As mentioned in Chapter One, these "ghost" lights appear almost nightly among nearby mountain peaks, dancing and hovering in endless, random patterns. Some observers feel that they are UFOs and that the mountains around Marfa may be some kind of extraterrestrial base of operations.

On January 2, 2007, while on the way to investigate the Coyame UFO crash, the authors of this book stopped for an evening's observation of Marfa's strange lights. What we saw there totally amazed us. As dusk descended upon the nearby Chinati mountain range, a series of unusual sparks of light started to twinkle along the tops of the Chinati mountain peaks. The lights slowly grew in intensity, sparkled, and then suddenly "winked out." Sometimes, we saw only one or two lights. Other times, we counted eight, nine, or ten all flickering along the mountaintops at once.

The eerie sight of the Marfa Lights continued for several hours and was later visible even from the parking lot of our motel, located about five miles west of the Texas Highway Department's official Marfa Lights "viewing area." Ruben Uriarte, who had never before witnessed the phenomenon, said, "This is one of the most amazing things I've ever witnessed."

Whatever strange goings-on are taking place in the skies along the Rio Grande River, it is possible that the U.S. military's tethered aerostat radar stations are carefully collecting data on them. Although it is likely that the general public will never see the data collected, one can always hope for a breakthrough someday, such as happened when the Deneb Report surfaced, telling the incredible tale of a UFO crash retrieval within a few miles of the Texas-Mexico border.

EPILOGUE

Why Mexico? The events described in this book happened on Mexico's side of its boundary with the United States. People often ask me why Mexico has been the site of some of the most dramatic and remarkable UFO sightings, especially in recent years. I think I may have at least part of the answer.

It has been my good fortune to visit many UFO hot spots in Mexico over the past few years and to talk to many Mexican UFO investigators and eyewitnesses. My interest in the Mexico UFO experience began in the mid-1990s, when I served as researcher, guide, and translator for *Beyond Boundaries*, a tour company that took people to areas of high UFO activity throughout the world, including Mexico.

It was in a small, isolated village near Mexico's active volcano Popocatépetl in 1996 that I came face-to-face with an experience that profoundly affected me. As I took notes furiously, a young boy named Claudio told a spellbinding tale about the day in 1993 that he encountered something beyond belief while herding goats in the hills near his home.

The boy, who had little formal education, almost no contact with the outside world, and no access to television, explained that, while tending the goats, he saw flash of light on a rocky ledge above him. The goats became frightened and gathered themselves together in a protective circle.

Looking up, Claudio saw three small humanoid beings with large heads standing on the ledge from which the bright light had emanated. The creatures wore tight-fitting clothes, and one of them had a growth of fine hair on his chin that looked like a beard. Although they did not speak by moving their mouths, Claudio could hear their thoughts in his mind.

The beings told Claudio that they had come to the area of Popocatépetl to keep the volcano from erupting. They indicated that their mission was especially important because there was a group of malignant beings, which they referred to as "the others," who were trying to cause Popocatépetl to erupt. During their telepathic link with Claudio, the beings also revealed to him a future world event that caused him great puzzlement.

161

The "bearded" creature said that there would be a "small war" in a place called New York. As Claudio was not well educated and had never been outside his village, he did not know anything about New York. The being also revealed that the "small war" would cause the entire world to go "on alert."

Claudio, The Boy Who Saw Entities (1996 Photo By Ruben Uriarte)

When I interviewed Claudio in 1996, I thought the beings were referring to the first terrorist attempt to blow up the World Trade Center in 1993. Obviously, after 2001, my assessment of the mysterious prophecy delivered to Claudio was forever changed. It is clear to me now that the beings were foretelling the horrendous destruction of the World Trade Center on September 11, 2001.

This is one of many unusual experiences I have had while traveling in Mexico. As many other people have come forward in recent years with similar strange tales, I am sometimes asked, "Why do you think Mexico is one of the world's most active regions for UFO sightings and other paranormal activity?" What follows is my response to this question.

History & Culture

Mystery shrouds much of the country's earliest history, but

162

evidence suggests that tribes of hunter-gatherers inhabited the land perhaps as early as 28,000 years before Christ. Ancient Mexicans began to selectively breed corn plants around 8,000 BC, create extensive pottery by 2,300 BC, and undertake large farming projects by about 1,800 BC.

Arising around 2,300 BC in the area now known as Veracruz, the Olmecs are generally viewed as Mexico's first great civilization. The Olmecs are said to have set the tone for all future Mexican cultures through their devotion to art, mathematics, astronomy, and religious mysticism. Known for carving mammoth stone heads, the Olmecs held complex spiritual beliefs based around several deities. Their achievements in art, science, and religion were passed on to later civilizations, including the Maya.

Mexico witnessed the rise of the great Teotihuacan culture in about 300 BC near what is now Mexico City. The center of culture and power was the great city of Teotihuacan, which by 150 AD was North America's first true "metropolis" and by 500 AD was the largest city in the world. A place steeped in mysticism, Teotihuacan was known as the "city where men become gods." Its inhabitants are known for building an impressive array of religious temples and structures. Two of the world's most amazing archeological wonders, the Pyramids of the Sun and the Moon, still stand today and are among Mexico's foremost tourist attractions.

Mexico's great Maya civilization may have begun as early as 1,000 BC, but it flourished between 250 and 650 AD, even as Teotihuacan was also at its height. Mayan innovations in mathematics, astronomy, and writing established the basis of Mexican scientific thought. Considered the most technologically advanced of pre-Columbian civilizations, the Maya built great cities, temples, pyramids, and other archaeological wonders. They are known for their complex religious beliefs, including their view of time as cyclical. In addition, they devoted a great deal of thought and effort to a careful study of the stars and planets.

An incredible Mayan artifact that survives today is the *Dresden Codex*, which ended up in Europe after Spain's conquest of Mexico. Written between 1000 and 1200 AD and totaling 74 pages, this amazing document contains detailed astronomical and astrological information, including prophecies pertaining to the end of the world.

Some researchers say that, in accurately predicting the total solar eclipse over Mexico on July 11, 1991, the codex speaks of a new age for mankind, characterized by major changes to the earth and an increasing number of encounters with mysterious beings referred to as "Masters of the Stars."

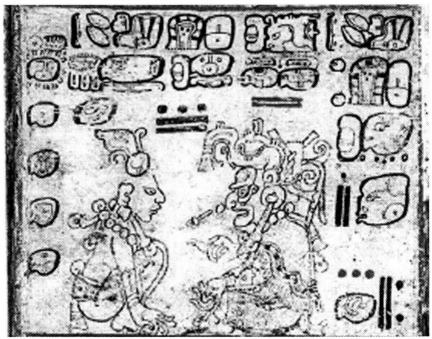

Portion of the Mayan Dresden Codex, Which Speaks of Unearthly Beings Called "Masters of the Stars" (Wikipedia Photo)

Mayan references to visitors from other worlds are found in the *Sixth Sun* prophecies written in 755 AD. One prophecy states, "In the era of the Sixth Sun, all that was buried will be discovered. Truth shall be the seed of life and the sons of the Sixth Sun will be the ones who travel through the stars."

Mexico's next great civilization after the Maya were the Toltecs, who became predominant in about 700 AD and were, in turn, followed by the powerful Aztec empire of the 1400s. Both of these peoples carried on the tradition of elaborate expressions of religious mysticism incorporating elements of the paranormal. Aztec rituals included the sacrifice of human victims, whose still-beating hearts

164

were ripped out and offered up to the sun. When the Spaniards invaded in 1519, the religious beliefs and traditions of Roman Catholicism were appended to the existing belief systems of the indigenous populations of Mexico, creating an odd mixture that continues to this day.

Many students of Mexico's past have suggested that the country's ancient inhabitants may have been visited by unearthly creatures from beyond the stars that descended in vessels of fire and imparted the wisdom that helped sustain the great civilizations of the Mayas and Aztecs. These strange visitors may be represented in some of the art and architecture of Mexico's past, and their existence may explain the obsession with astronomy of even the earliest Mexican civilizations.

Geography & Isolation

Another factor contributing to the high incidence of UFO activity in Mexico may be simply a matter of geography. The country has vast areas of pristine wilderness, including numerous mountain ranges, foremost of which are the Sierra Madre Occidental and the Sierra Madre Oriental. In addition, two giant desert regions, the Chihuahuan and the Sonoran, dominate a huge portion of Northern Mexico. Dense tropical forests are found in the country's southern zones. This incredibly diverse landscape has resulted in an equally diverse and complex array of plant and animal life distributed throughout the country.

Since extraterrestrials are believed by some to hold a special fondness for the study of earth's animal and plant resources, Mexico seems to offer unlimited opportunities for such scientific research, while also affording isolation due to its vast expanses of sparsely populated wilderness areas. Some UFO researchers have suggested that Mexico's rugged mountains and isolated deserts may also serve as ideal locations for UFO occupants to establish secret bases from which to conduct their activities here on earth.

Also, there may be a connection between UFOs and some of Mexico's most unusual geographical formations, such as the awe-inspiring twin volcanoes, Popocatépetl and Iztaccíhuatl, located near Mexico City. Recent intense UFO activity around Popocatépetl, for example, has led many people to believe that the unearthly spacecraft may be conducting research on it or may even be somehow keeping it from erupting and endangering the lives of millions of people who live in the volcano's shadow.

Safety Zone

If UFO pilots are concerned about being intercepted and harassed by the planet's predominant military power, the United States, it stands to reason that they would choose Mexico as a much safer place to fly. Mexican air space is much more accessible, protected by an air force and an air defense system that is less threatening than that of the United States. In fact, while there have been numerous reports of UFOs being pursued, intercepted, and even shot down in the United States, no such cases have ever been confirmed in Mexico.

It is a safe assumption based on observed behavior that UFOs wish to remain hidden. This goal is much more easily accomplished in Mexico, with its still-developing infrastructure of technology, communications, and other public services. Large areas of Mexico remain unserved by the modern conveniences and technologies that most Americans and Europeans take for granted.

In addition to Mexico being a relative "safe zone" for UFO visitors, it offers the added benefit of being right on the doorstep of the world's greatest example of a modern, technological superpower, the United States. From the relative safety and isolation of Mexico's rugged, unexplored wilderness areas, UFOs may roam freely, making quick missions for surveillance and data gathering into the much more hostile and dangerous U.S. territories.

Conclusion

Regardless of what their specific interest in Mexico might be, UFOs have increased their activity within the country to an amazing degree since 1991. The explosion of sightings and evidence cannot be ignored, and neither can one ignore the profound influence UFOs are having on society both in Mexico and in its giant neighbor to the north.

Mexico's history of UFO activity has found its way into the U.S. media, including several major UFO-related motion pictures. Steven Spielberg's transcendent 1977 classic *Close Encounters of the Third Kind* opens with the aftermath of a massive UFO event in the Sonoran Desert of Northwestern Mexico. "The sun came out last night," a Mexican villager says in Spanish, "And it sang to me."

One of Spielberg's inspirations was Rod Serling's *Twilight Zone* television series, which in 1962 featured an episode about a UFO crash in a tiny Mexican village just across the Texas-Mexico border. Written by Serling, "The Gift" tells the story of an extraterrestrial in human form who has come to earth to share an amazing gift that will bring an end to all forms of cancer. Unfortunately, the narrow-minded, superstitious villagers persecute the stranger and end up killing him and destroying the gift.

In M. Night Shyamalan's *Signs*, a 2002 film about an attempted alien invasion of earth, a foreshadowing of what is to come occurs early in the movie, when a formation of strange lights appears in the skies over Mexico City. Later, the people of earth get their first look at the blurry figure of an alien from a homemade video shot in South America. The video looks strikingly similar to footage shot by residents in and around Mexico City during the UFO flap of the mid-1990s.

As even the U.S. media recognizes the significance of Mexico's role in the UFO experience, an explosion of interest in flying saucers continues to sweep both countries. It is within this context that we have examined, in this book, some of the strangest of all the Mexican UFO cases, the reported crash retrievals of unidentified flying objects along the U.S.–Mexico border.

Ruben J. Uriarte
Union City, California
March 6, 2007

AFTERWARD

UFO Crash Retrievals and Leaked Documents
By Stanton T. Friedman

By their very nature, investigations into crashed flying saucers and leaked government documents about UFOs are extremely difficult, frustrating, time-consuming and expensive. In such a wasteland of adversity, one revels in the joy of occasionally finding the latest piece of an ever-unfolding puzzle. I myself have lived this drama, as I am the nuclear physicist who first investigated the Roswell UFO crash in the early 1970s and later saw the investigation move into high gear after I located and interviewed Major Jesse Marcel and other key witnesses in 1978. My search for truth continued in the 1980s, as I personally visited twenty different document archives seeking information about the controversial *Majestic 12* documents, which are said to be leaked top secret documents about a government conspiracy to hide the existence of UFOs. As I often tell journalists, the problem with UFO research is not a lack of data, but rather an over-abundance of it. How can legitimate researchers effectively find their way through such a conflicting maze of information?

Mixed into the equation are the efforts of a loud community of noisy negativists who attack all aspects of UFO research, especially crash retrieval cases and leaked documents like *Majestic 12*. As a rule, these naysayers take full advantage of the four basic rules for debunkers:

1. *Don't bother me with the facts, because my mind is made up.*
2. *What the public doesn't know, I won't tell them.*
3. *If one can't attack the data, attack the person presenting the data - which is much easier anyway.*
4. *Do your research by proclamation, because investigation is too much trouble, and besides, most people won't know the difference.*

One such group is the *Committee for the Scientific Investigation of Claims of the Paranormal*, which categorically denies all "paranormal" explanations for UFOs. Their chief "scientific" investigator is Dr. Joseph Nickell, a full-time employee of the group, whose credibility rests on three college degrees in English. Nickell has had a long involvement in professional deception by magical sleight of hand.

In a television interview featuring Nickell in Los Angeles and me in Roswell, he attempted to explain away the Roswell incident by proclaiming, with no evidence at all, that the public affairs officer at the Roswell Air Base fabricated the story for attention. When I asked if he even knew that officer's name, he replied, "Well, no." I pointed out that the man in question, Walter Haut, was anything but a publicity seeker. Haut was a bombardier on more than twenty missions over Japan, had been chosen to drop a very important instrument package during the *Operation Crossroads* nuclear tests in the Pacific in 1946, and was highly esteemed in the town of Roswell for his involvement in community affairs. Haut belonged to the 509th Army Bomb Group, which was the most elite military group in the world in 1947, having successfully carried out the nuclear weapon drops on Hiroshima and Nagasaki in 1945. The notion that Haut would deliberately fake a press release about a captured UFO to draw attention to himself is absurd. Unlike Nickell, I took the time to get to know Haut. I had been in his home. We shared several meals together. He was not just an abstract concept to me.

Nickell further demonstrated his poor research skills when he attacked the Top Secret, Eyes Only *Eisenhower Briefing Document*, which discusses the crash at Roswell and the establishment of *Operation Majestic 12* and briefly notes the Del Rio crash. Nickell declared confidently that the document was fraudulent because the date format "18 November, 1952" violated the government style manual. Yet, during many visits to the Eisenhower and Truman Libraries and other archives, I found that many different date formats were in use during the early 1950s. Two different members of Majestic 12, CIA Directors Roscoe H. Hillenkoetter and Walter B. Smith, used the format in question. I found many different date formats in definitely genuine documents of the time period.

Underscoring this point, I have often cited three authentic, verified letters from CIA director Allen Dulles to Eisenhower's Staff Secretary, Andrew Goodpaster, which were written within a ten-day period in 1956 and which used three different date formats[1].

Another skeptic, the late Karl Pflock, believed that aliens visit the earth and that they abducted Betty and Barney Hill, but, oddly, he steadfastly denied the validity of Roswell and *Majestic 12*. As stated in his book, *Inconvenient Facts and the Will to Believe*[2], Pflock's objections include the use of the old and still false notion that absence of evidence means evidence of absence. He could not find any relevant evidence in the few documents he reviewed; therefore, none existed! He asserted that some people considered Colonel Blanchard, head of the 509th, a "loose cannon" who might have approved the Roswell UFO press release to further his personal ambitions. The Eisenhower Library, as of three years ago, still had 300,000 classified documents. Blanchard had four promotions after the Roswell event to four-star General. He had been chief of operations for the Strategic Air Command, Inspector General of the United States Air Force and was Vice Chief of Staff of the Air Force when he died of a massive heart attack in 1966. Some loose cannon!

Pflock also dismissed the story of Roswell pilot Pappy Henderson having handled wreckage and seen alien bodies because Henderson was supposedly a practical joker who had tried to pass off a piece of a V-2 rocket as Roswell wreckage to various people including a friend, dentist John Kromshroeder. I later met with Kromshroeder, who came forward only after the broadcast of the *Unsolved Mysteries* program about Roswell in 1989. Len Stringfield, who published monographs including more than sixty crashed saucer stories he had collected (he rarely did any in-depth investigation), had written an article in the *MUFON (Mutual UFO Network) Journal* telling of a conversation with Henderson's wife, Sappho. She said Henderson claimed to have seen wreckage and alien bodies. Thanks to the producers of *Unsolved Mysteries*, I was later able to locate and talk to Sappho. She gave me the names of five people with whom her late husband had discussed Roswell. Afterward, I was able to contact all of them.

Stringfield also wrote about an alleged Cape Girardeau, Missouri, UFO crash recovery in 1942, as told by Charlette Mann, granddaughter of Reverend Huffman, who had supposedly given last rites to an alien. Again there was no validation. Mrs. Stringfield, after her husband's death, would not check his files to find contact information for Charlette. With considerable effort, I was able to find not just people who had known Reverend Huffman, but also Charlette herself. I even located the photographer who received a print of a photograph taken of the alien's body.

Turning back to the Roswell crash, Dr. Kevin Randle says "yes" to the Roswell event[3], but "no"[4] to *Operation Majestic 12*. He even wrote an entire book attacking the Majestic documents[5]. In my lengthy review of that book and at my website *www.stantonfriedman.com*, I proved that none of his arguments held up[6]. His main objection to the *Eisenhower Briefing Document* is that the briefing officer is identified as "Admiral" Roscoe H. Hillenkoetter; whereas Hillenkoetter was actually only a rear admiral and would never have signed as "Admiral." However, it is important to note that Hillenkoetter did not sign his name anywhere on the document and therefore clearly did not attribute the title of "Admiral" to himself. For clerical staff at the time, it was standard practice to use generic ranks for military personnel, as was also done for the other military members of MJ-12. At the Eisenhower Presidential Library, I myself found a number of *memcons* (memos of conversation) by General Andrew Goodpaster listing the attendees at various White House meetings and notes about the meetings. The ranks given in the list, including his, were "general" or "admiral," although very few of them actually had four stars. He signed the memos *Brigadier General* Goodpaster. Two archivists later told me that the use of generic ranks was standard practice at that time.

Randle claimed correctly that I found nothing in the Menzel papers at Harvard that referred to or hinted at there being an *Operation Majestic 12* of which astronomer Donald Menzel was said to be a member. I determined (after getting written permission from three people to see Menzel's papers at Harvard) to my great surprise that Menzel had been engaged in very highly classified intelligence work for many decades with a top secret clearance from the National Security Agency and the Central Intelligence Agency. He also worked on classified matters for several large companies. Of course there were no classified papers at all in his Harvard files., because, as someone highly knowledgeable in the proper handling of classified documents, he would not have put them there.

In the second edition of my book *Top Secret/MAJIC* [7], I deal with numerous unjustifiable attacks on the Majestic documents. I also point out in the book and in other papers[8] specific false claims against the legitimate documents and demonstrate that a host of fraudulent documents have also been put forth as received by Tim Cooper. Dealing with both the hoaxed documents and the legitimate ones takes a lot of hard work, which is something the debunkers almost never do.

A case in point is the July 14, 1954, *Cutler-Twining Memo* from Eisenhower's national security advisor, Robert Cutler, to General Nathan F. Twining, a supposed MJ-12 member, Chief of Staff of the Air Force, and later Chairman of the Joint Chiefs. William Moore and Jaime Shandera found the memo in Box 189 at the National Archives of Entry 267, Record Group 341, in July 1985. This is a brief original *TOP SECRET RESTRICTED* onion skin carbon document whose subject is the provocative "NSC/MJ-12 Special Studies Project Briefing." In my writings, I review a host of attacks against the validity of this document. Philip Klass claimed that the memo should have been typed in a small elite typeface rather than large Pica typeface, based on all of *nine* other NSC documents he examined. Despite the fact that he had never been to the Eisenhower Library, he challenged me to provide any other genuine pica type documents from the same office and time frame and offered me $100 each, up to a maximum of ten. I provided fourteen documents that met all of his criteria, and he was forced to pay me $1,000. A copy of the check and correspondence is available in my publications. Obviously, it was very unreasonable for him to generalize from the nine documents he looked at to the 250,000 pages of NSC materials at the Eisenhower Presidential Library.

Many armchair theorists complain that the Cutler-Twining memo used the "fraudulent" security marking *TOP SECRET/ RESTRICTED*. However, the General Accounting office in its search for Roswell documents, stated, "In several instances we noticed the classification Top Secret Restricted used on several documents. This is mentioned because in past references to this classification (Majestic 12), we were told that it was not used during this period."

The original of the *Cutler-Twining Memo*, when held up to a window, reveals a watermark that allowed us to trace the company that made the paper, in bid lots only, and in the right time frame. The government bought much of this paper, and it was not sold in stationery stores. There is also a slant red pencil mark through the security marking, a little known standard practice when a document was to be declassified. Xerox copies do not show either the red color or the watermark.

Some critics loudly complain that all Top Secret documents had to have Top Secret Control Numbers, none of which appear on the MJ-12 documents. Nonetheless, I have found and reprinted a number of other legitimate documents that did not have control numbers, and an archivist from the Eisenhower Library told me that their records included had many Top Secret documents without control numbers[9].

Research on crashed saucers, as with these leaked documents, has many pitfalls and problems. I was lucky with regard to Roswell. I had stories from Lydia Sleppy and Jesse Marcel. Bill Moore had a story from a United Kingdom publication, the *Flying Saucer Review*, about a British actor, Hughie Green, who heard the crash story on the radio while driving from Los Angeles to Philadelphia. He estimated the date as late June or early July 1947. Moore went to the University of Minnesota library in 1978 and found the newspaper stories from July 8, 1947. Eventually, we found them in other papers from Chicago and elsewhere. The articles yielded the names of other individuals involved in the Roswell case and validated what Marcel had told me. I checked telephone information and found Bill Brazel, son of rancher Mac. He had just obtained a phone two weeks earlier. I found in *Editor and Publisher* a listing for the *Roswell Daily Record*, called and mentioned an article talking about the base public information officer, Walter Haut. To my astonishment, I was told that his wife worked at the paper. Walter had a base yearbook, knew Blanchard very well, and was a big help. I thought that General Ramey and Colonel DuBose, who were in pictures that I obtained from the *Fort Worth Star Telegram* of July 8, 1947, were likely graduated from West Point, and it turned out that they were, as was Blanchard. DuBose, a retired general, was still alive, and I found him extremely helpful when I visited with him in Florida. In two years, we had located sixty-two people connected with the Roswell Incident, although some did not know much about the event. A letter to the *Socorro Daily Chieftain* seeking people who had known Barney Barnett of the Plains of San Agustin crash brought forth a former neighbor to whom Barney had briefly told his story shortly before dying of cancer. Other who had known Barnett were also located. Fortunately, almost all of the early research was done before *The Roswell Incident* was published in 1980, and thus was not adversely influenced by the meddlesome media circus that resulted afterward.

I, and other researchers, also located other people connected with Roswell who told good stories that either could not be verified or made no sense. One woman claimed her father was a Roswell fireman and went out to the crash site with a fire department vehicle. Others said that this was unlikely because it would have left Roswell unprotected during the scorching summer. The woman also claimed that a State Highway patrolman gave her a piece of UFO "memory metal" to play with. In a state as security conscious as New Mexico, this also seems highly unlikely.

Frank Kaufmann, who was Kevin Randle's star witness for some time (though now completely discredited even by Randle), said all kinds of things that made no sense. He claimed to have come back to town from White Sands and awakened Colonel Blanchard and Jesse Marcel in the middle of the night, early July 6, to go to a crash site on the Corn ranch. He said he called the base, and a flatbed truck was sent out, picked up the wreckage and bodies, and was back at the base by morning. However, the terrain, according to the landowners, had no road and was accessible only by horseback. Also, Marcel and Blanchard surely would have reacted differently if they had already seen bodies and wreckage when rancher Brazel came to town later that same day. Blanchard would not have left the base without knowing what was found.

Locating witnesses to a UFO event was certainly much more difficult before the Internet. When investigating Roswell, among my best sources were the Christmas lists of the wives of the military men stationed at Roswell. Another useful source were the professional organizations to which Roswell-connected individuals belonged. For example, meteorologist Irving Newton, based in Fort Worth in July 1947 and shown in a picture taken in General Ramey's office, was listed in the membership records of the American Meteorology Society.

If a former military man claims to have been at a certain specific post during a UFO event, one may check his *DD 214* discharge papers. If he claims to have graduated from a college, one can check with that institution's registrar or alumni association. It is amazing how many lies I have caught this way, as in the case of infamous UFO hoaxer Bob Lazar, who claimed to have earned Master's degrees in Physics from the Massachusetts Institute of Technology and in electronics from California Institute of Technology. He also stated that he had been a scientist with Los Alamos National Lab. Despite his claims, his name is nowhere to be found in the records of any of the relevant registrars, alumni groups, physics departments, commencements, et cetera. Neither MIT nor Cal Tech ever heard of him.

Lazar *was* in the phone book at the Los Alamos National Lab, but he was clearly identified as working for a subcontractor, not for the lab itself. Lazar also claimed that a certain professor, Dr. Bill Duxler of the Cal Tech Physics department, would remember him. But alas, Duxler never taught at Cal Tech. He did, however, teach at Pierce Junior College in Southern California, where records show that Lazar was actually enrolled at the very time he claimed to be at MIT, 2,500 miles away.

The point here is that UFO crash research is not easy and is fraught with obstacles that range from the difficulty of locating witnesses to the blanket of government deception that seems to constantly surface in these cases. Noe Torres and Ruben Uriarte are to be commended for taking on this task. They have the additional complication of having two countries involved. I hope that this book will encourage others to come forward with additional clues, first and second hand stories, and any pertinent data. Surely the recovery of crashed alien spacecraft is of great importance for understanding our place in the local galactic neighborhood, even if it proves that we are not the highly advanced civilization we would like to think we are and that earthly governments have willingly deceived us, probably out of a blind desire to maintain power and to exploit extraterrestrial technology for military purposes.

Stanton T. Friedman, Nuclear Physicist and
Original Researcher of the Roswell UFO Crash
September 2006

ENDNOTES

[1] Friedman, Stanton T. "Final Report on Operation Majestic 12" 1990, 105 pages. $10 including S&H from UFORI, POB 958, Houlton, ME 04730-0958.

[2] Pflock, Karl. *Roswell:Inconvenient Facts and the Will to Believe*, Prometheus Press, 2001, 331 pages.

[3] Randle, Kevin and Schmitt, Don. *UFO Crash at Roswell* Avon Paperback, 1991, 327 Pages.

[4] Randle, Kevin and Schmitt, Don. *The Truth About the UFO Crash at Roswell* 1994, M. Evans, 251 pages; Avon Paperback, 1994, 314 pages.

[5] Randle, Kevin. *Case MJ-12: The True Story Behind the Government's UFO Conspiracies*, paperback Harper Collins, December , 2002, 311 pages.

[6] Friedman, Stanton T. "Review of Case MJ-12 by K.D. Randle". January 2003, 27p. $4 from UFORI.

[7] Friedman, Stanton T. *Top Secret/MAJIC*, Marlowe and Company 2nd Edition, 2005, 282pg. $17 from UFORI.

[8] Friedman, Stanton T. "Roswell and the MJ-12 Documents in the New Millennium" 2000, 29 pages, 20 References. $4.UFORI.

[9] Friedman, Stanton T. "Majestic 12 Documents Update"April 2004 26 p. from UFORI.

177

SUBJECT: THE CHIHUAHUA DISK CRASH

To: All Deneb Team Members
From: JS
Date: 23 Mar 92
Subject: Research Findings on the Chihuahua Disk Crash
Text:

On 25 Aug 74, at 2207 hrs, US Air Defense radar detected an unknown approaching US airspace from the Gulf of Mexico. Originally the object was tracked at 2,200 (2530 mph) knots on a bearing of 325 degrees and at an altitude of 75,000 feet, a course that would intercept US territory about forty miles southwest of Corpus Christi, Texas. After approximately sixty seconds of observation, at a position 155 miles southeast of Corpus Christi, the object simultaneously decelerated to approximately 1700 (1955 mph) knots, turned to a heading of 290 degrees, and began a slow descent. It entered Mexican airspace approximately forty miles south of Brownsville, Texas. Radar tracked it approximately 500 miles to a point near the town of Coyame, in the state of Chihuahua, not far from the US border. There the object suddenly disappeared from the radar screens.

During the flight over Mexican airspace, the object leveled off at 45,000 feet, then descended to 20,000 feet. The descent was in level steps, not a smooth curve or straight line, and each level was maintained for approximately five minutes.

The object was tracked by two different military radar installations. It would have been within range of Brownsville civilian radar, but it is assumed that no civilian radar detected the object due to a lack of any such reports. The point of disappearance from the radar screens was over a barren and sparsely populated area of Northern Mexico. At first it was assumed that the object had

178

descended below the radar's horizon and a watch was kept for any re-emergence of the object. None occurred.

At first it was assumed that the object might be a meteor because of the high speed and descending flight path. But meteors normally travel at higher speeds, and descend in a smooth arc, not in "steps." And meteors do not normally make a thirty-five degree change in course. Shortly after detection an air defense alert was called. However, before any form of interception could be scrambled, the object turned to a course that would not immediately take it over US territory. The alert was called off within twenty minutes after the object's disappearance from the radar screen.

Fifty-two minutes after the disappearance, civilian radio traffic indicated that a civilian aircraft had gone down in that area. But it was clear that the missing aircraft had departed El Paso International with a destination of Mexico City, and could not, therefore, have been the object tracked over the Gulf of Mexico.

It was noted, however, that they both disappeared in the same area and at the same time.

With daylight the next day, Mexican authorities began a search for the missing plane. Approximately 1035 hrs there came a radio report that wreckage from the missing plane had been spotted from the air. Almost immediately came a report of a second plane on the ground a few miles from the first. A few minutes later an additional report stated that the second "plane" was circular shaped and apparently in one piece although damaged. A few minutes after that the Mexican military clamped a radio silence on all search efforts.

The radio interceptions were reported through channels to the CIA. Possibly as many as two additional government agencies also received reports, but such has not been confirmed as of this date. The CIA immediately began forming a recovery team. The speed with which this team and its equipment was assembled suggests that this was either a well-rehearsed exercise or one that had been performed prior to this event.

In the meantime requests were initiated at the highest levels between the United States and Mexican governments that the US recovery team be allowed onto Mexican territory to "assist." These requests were met with professed ignorance and a flat refusal of any cooperation.

By 2100 hrs [1200 hrs?], 26 Aug 74, the recovery team had assembled and been staged at Fort Bliss. Several helicopters were flown in from some unknown source and assembled in a secured area. These helicopters were painted a neutral sand color and bore no markings. Eye witness indicates that there were three smaller craft, very probably UHl Hueys from the description. There was also a larger helicopter, possibly a Sea Stallion. Personnel from this team remained with their craft and had no contact with other Ft. Bliss personnel.

Satellite and recognizance aircraft overflight that day indicated that both the crashed disk and the civilian aircraft had been removed from the crash sites and loaded on flat bed trucks. Later flights confirmed that the convoy had departed the area heading south.

At that point the CIA had to make a choice, either to allow this unknown aircraft to stay in the hands of the Mexican government, or to launch the recovery team, supplemented by any required military support, to take the craft. There occurred, however, an event that took the choice out of their hands. High altitude overflights indicated that the convoy had stopped before reaching any inhabited areas or major roads. Recon showed no activity, and radio contact between the Mexican recovery team and its headquarters had ceased. A low altitude, high-speed overflight was ordered.

The photos returned by that aircraft showed all trucks and jeeps stopped, some with open doors, and two human bodies laying on the ground beside two vehicles. The decision was immediately made to launch the recovery team but the actual launching was held up for the arrival of additional equipment and two additional personnel. It was not until 1438 hrs that the helicopters departed Ft. Bliss.

The four helicopters followed the border down towards Presidio then turned and entered Mexican airspace north of Candelaria. They were over the convoy site at 1653 hrs. All convoy personnel were dead, most within the trucks. Some recovery team members, dressed bio-protection suits, reconfigured the straps holding the object on the flatbed truck, then attached them to a cargo cable from the Sea Stallion. By 1714 hrs the recovered object was on its way to US territory. Before leaving the convoy site, members of the recovery team gathered together the Mexican vehicles and bodies, then destroyed all with high explosives. This included the pieces of the civilian light plane which had been involved in the mid-air collision. At 1746 hrs the Hueys departed.

The Hueys caught up with the Sea Stallion as it reentered US airspace. The recovery team then proceeded to a point in the Davis Mountains, approximately twenty-five miles north east of Valentine. There they landed and waited until 0225 hrs the next morning. At that time they resumed the flight and rendezvoused with a small convoy on a road between Van Horn and Kent. The recovered disk was transferred to a truck large enough to handle it and capable of being sealed totally. Some of the personnel from the Huey's transferred to the convoy.

All helicopters then returned to their original bases for decontamination procedures. The convoy continued non-stop, using back roads and smaller highways, and staying away from cities. The destination of the convoy reportedly was Altanta, Georgia.

Here the hard evidence thins out. One unconfirmed report says the disk was eventually transferred to Wright-Patterson AF Base. Another says that the disk was either transferred after that to another unnamed base, or was taken directly to this unknown base directly from Atlanta.

The best description of the disk was that it was sixteen feet, five inches in diameter, convex on both upper and lower surfaces to the same degree, possessing no visible doors or windows. The thickness was slightly less than five feet. The color was silver, much like polished steel. There were no visible lights nor any propulsion means. There were no markings. There were two areas of the rim that showed damage, one showing an irregular hole approximately twelve inches in diameter with indented material around it. The other damage was described as a "dent" about two feet wide. The weight of the object was estimated as approximately one thousand, five hundred pounds, based on the effect of the weight on the carrying helicopter and those who transferred it to the truck.

There was no indication in the documentation available as to whether anything was visible in the "hole."

It seems likely that the damage with the hole was caused by the collision with the civilian aircraft. That collision occurred while the object was traveling approximately 1700 knots (1955 mph). Even ignoring the speed of the civilian aircraft, the impact would have been considerable at that speed. This is in agreement with the description of the civilian aircraft as being "almost totally destroyed." What was being taken from the crash site was pieces of the civilian aircraft.

The second damage may have resulted when the object impacted with the ground. The speed in that case should have been considerably less than that of the first impact.

No mention is made of the occupants of the civilian aircraft. It is not known if any body or bodies were recovered. Considering the destruction of the civilian light aircraft in mid-air, bodies may well not have come down near the larger pieces.

Unfortunately what caused the deaths of the Mexican recovery team is not known. Speculation ranges from a chemical released from the disk as a result of the damage, to a microbiological agent. There are no indications of death or illness by any of the recovery team. It would not have been illogical for the recovery team to have taken one of the bodies back with them for analysis. But there is no indication of that having happen. Perhaps they did not have adequate means of transporting what might have been a biologically contaminated body.

Inquires to the FAA reveal no documents concerning the civilian aircraft crash, probably because it did not involve a US aircraft.

It should be noted that the above facts do not tell the complete story. Nothing is known of the analysis of the craft or its contents. Nothing is known about the deaths associated with the foreign recovery team. Nor is it known if this craft was manned or not.

Other questions also remain, such as why would a recovered disk be taken to Altanta? And where did the disk come from? It was first detected approximately 200 miles from US territory, yet US air defenses extend to a much greater distance than that. If the object descended into the atmosphere, perhaps NORAD space tracking has some record of the object. Alternate possibility is that it entered the Gulf of Mexico under radar limits then "jumped" up to 75,000 feet. Considering prior behavior exhibited by disks of this size, it is probable that the entry was from orbital altitude.

The facts that are known have been gathered from two eye witness accounts, documentation illegally copied, and a partially destroyed document. This was done in 1978 by a person who is now dead. Only in February of this year [1992] did the notes and documents come into the hands of our group.

END OF DOCUMENT

Appendix B: Report of the Scientific Panel on Unidentified Flying Objects (1953)

1. Pursuant to the request of the Assistant Director for Scientific Intelligence, the undersigned Panel of Scientific Consultants has met to evaluate any possible threat to national security posed by Unidentified Flying Objects ("Flying Saucers"), and to make recommendations thereon. The Panel has received the evidence as presented by cognizant intelligence agencies, primarily the Air Technical Intelligence Center, and has reviewed a selection of the best documented incidents.

2. As a result of its considerations, the Panel concludes:

a.) That the evidence presented on Unidentified Flying Objects shows no indication that these phenomena constitute a direct physical threat to national security.

We firmly believe that there is no residuum of cases which indicates phenomena which are attributable to foreign artifacts capable of hostile acts, and that there is no evidence that the phenomena indicates a need for the revision of current scientific concepts.

3. The Panel further concludes:

a.) That the continued emphasis on the reporting of these phenomena does, in these perilous times, result in a threat to the orderly functioning of the protective organs of the body politic.

We cite as examples the clogging of channels of communication by irrelevant reports, the danger of being led by continued false alarms to ignore real indications of hostile action, and the cultivation of a morbid national psychology in which skillful hostile propaganda could induce hysterical behavior and harmful distrust of duty constituted authority.

4. In order most effectively to strengthen the national facilities for the timely recognition and the appropriate handling of true indications of hostile action, and to minimize the concomitant dangers alluded to above, the Panel recommends:

a.) That the national security agencies take immediate steps to strip the Unidentified Flying Objects of the special status they have been given and the aura of mystery they have unfortunately acquired;

b.) That the national security agencies institute policies on intelligence, training, and public education designed to prepare the material defenses and the morale of the country to recognize most promptly and to react most effectively to true indications of hostile intent or action.

We suggest that these aims may be achieved by an integrated program designed to reassure the public of the total lack of evidence of inimical forces behind the phenomenon, to train personnel to recognize and reject false indications quickly and effectively, and to strengthen regular channels for the evaluation of and prompt reaction to true indications of hostile measures.

/s/ Lloyd V. Berkner
Associated Universities, Inc.

/s/ H.P. Robertson, Chairman
California Institute of Technology

/s/ S. A. Goudsmit
Brookhaven National Laboratories

/s/ Luis W. Alvarez
University of California

/s/ Thornton Page
Johns Hopkins University

APPENDIX C: THE EISENHOWER
BRIEFING DOCUMENT (EBD)

Subject: Operation Majestic-12 Preliminary Briefing for President-Elect Eisenhower -- Document Prepared 18 November, 1952.

Briefing Officer: Adm. Roscoe H. Hillenkoetter (MJ-1)

OPERATION MAJESTIC-12 is a TOP SECRET Research and Development/Intelligence operation responsible directly and only to the President of the United States. Operations of the project are carried out under control of the Majestic-12 (Majic-12) Group which was established by special classified executive order of President Truman on 24 September, 1947, upon recommendation by Dr. Vannevar Bush and Secretary James Forrestal. (See Attachment "A".) Members of the majestic-12 Group were designated as follows: Adm. Roscoe H. Hillenkoetter, Dr. Vannevar Bush, Secy. James V. Forrestal, Gen. Nathan F. Twining, Gen. Hoyt S. Vandenberg, Dr. Detlev Bronk, Dr. Jerome Hunsaker, Mr. Sidney W. Souers, Mr. Gordon Gray, Dr. Donald Menzel, Gen. Robert M. Montague, Dr. Lloyd V. Berkner.

The death of Secretary Forrestal on 22 May, 1949, created a vacancy which remained unfilled until 01 August, 1950, upon which date Gen. Walter B. Smith was designated as permanent replacement.

On 24 June, 1947, a civilian pilot, flying over the Cascade Mountains in the State of Washington observed nine flying disk-shaped aircraft traveling in formation at a high rate of speed. Although this was not the first known sighting of such objects, it was the first to gain widespread attention in the public media. Hundreds of reports of sightings of similar objects followed. Many of these came from highly credible military and civilian sources. These reports resulted in independent efforts by several different elements of the military to ascertain the nature and purpose of these objects in the interests of national defense. A number of witnesses were interviewed and there were several unsuccessful attempts to utilize aircraft in efforts to pursue reported discs in flight. Public reaction bordered on near hysteria at times.

In spite of these efforts, little of substance was learned about the objects until a local rancher reported that one had crashed in a remote region of New Mexico located approximately seventy-five miles northwest of Roswell Army Air Base (now Walker Field).

On 07 July, 1947, a secret operation was begun to assure recovery of the wreckage of this object for scientific study. During the course of this operation, aerial reconnaissance discovered that four small human-like beings had apparently ejected from the craft at some point before it exploded. These had fallen to earth about two miles east of the wreckage site. All four were dead and badly decomposed due to action by predators and exposure to the elements during the approximately one week time period which had elapsed before their discovery. A special scientific took charge of removing these bodies for study. (See Attachment "C".) The wreckage of the craft was also removed to several different locations. (See Attachment "B".) Civilian and military witnesses in the area were debriefed, and news reporters were given the effective cover story that the object had been a misguided weather research balloon.

A covert analytical effort organized by Gen. Twining and Dr. Bush acting on the direct orders of the President, resulted in a preliminary consensus (19 September, 1947) that the disk was most likely a short range reconnaissance craft. This conclusion was based for the most part on the craft's size and the apparent lack of any identifiable provisioning. (See Attachment "D".) A similar analysis of the four dead occupants was arranged by Dr. Bronk. It was the tentative conclusion of this group (30 November, 1947) that although these creatures are human-like in appearance, the biological and evolutionary processes responsible for their development has apparently been quite different from those observed or postulated in homo-sapiens. Dr Bronk's tea has suggested the term "Extra-terrestrial Biological Entities", or "EBEs", be adopted as the

187

standard term of reference for these creatures until such time as a more definitive designation can be agreed upon.

Since it is virtually certain that these craft do not originate in any country on earth, considerable speculation has centered around what their point of origin may be and how they get here. Mars was and remains a possibility, although some scientists, most notably Dr. Menzel, consider it more likely that we are dealing with beings from another solar system entirely.

Numerous examples of what appear to be a form of writing were found in the wreckage. Efforts to decipher these have remained largely unsuccessful. (See Attachment "E".) Equally unsuccessful have been efforts to determine the methods of propulsion or the nature or method of transmission of the power source involved. Research along these lines has been complicated by the complete absence of identifiable wings, propellers, jets, or other conventional methods of propulsion and guidance, as well as a total lack of metallic wiring, vacuum tubes, or similar recognizable electronic components. (See Attachment "F".) It is assumed that the propulsion unit was completely destroyed by the explosion which caused the crash.

A need for as much additional information as possible about these craft, their performance characteristics and their purpose led to the undertaking known as U.S. Air Force Project SIGN in December, 1947. In order to preserve security, liaison between SIGN and Majestic-12 was limited to two individuals within the Intelligence Division of Air Material Command whose role was to pass along certain types of information through channels. SIGN evolved into Project GRUDGE in December, 1948. The operation is currently being conducted under the code name BLUE BOOK, with liaison maintained through the Air Force officer who is head of the project.

On 06 December, 1950, a second object, probably of similar origin, impacted the earth at high speed in the El Indio - Guerrero area of Texas - Mexican border after following a long trajectory through the atmosphere. by the time a search team arrived, what remained of the object as been totally incinerated. Such material as could be recovered was transported to the A.E.C. facility at Sandia, New Mexico, for study.

Implications for the National Security are of continuing importance in that the motives and ultimate intentions of these visitors remain completely unknown. In addition, a significant upsurge in the surveillance activity of these craft beginning in May and continuing through the autumn of this year has caused considerable concern that new developments may be imminent. It is for these reasons, as well as the obvious international and technological considerations and the ultimate need to avoid a public panic at all costs, that the Majestic-12 Group remains of the unanimous opinion that imposition of the strictest security precautions should continue without interruption into the new administration. At the same time, contingency plan MJ-1949-04P/78 (Top Secret - Eyes Only) should be held in continued readiness should the need to make a public announcement present itself. (See Attachment "G".)

NOTE: The attachments were not included when this document surfaced in 1987.

APPENDIX D: LAW AGAINST EXTRATERRESTRIAL CONTACT (1969-1991)

1211.100 Title 14 - Aeronautics and Space
Part 1211 - Extra-terrestrial Exposure
1211.100 - Scope

This part establishes: (a) NASA policy, responsibility and authority to guard the Earth against any harmful contamination or adverse changes in its environment resulting from personnel, spacecraft and other property returning to the Earth after landing on or coming within the atmospheric envelope of a celestial body; and (b) security requirements, restrictions and safeguards that are necessary in the interest of national security.

1211.101 - Applicability

The provisions of this part to all NASA manned and unmanned space missions which land or come within the atmospheric envelope of a celestial body and return to the Earth.

1211.102 - Definitions

(a) "NASA" and the "Administrator" mean, respectively the National Aeronautics and Space Administration and the administrator of the National Aeronautics and Space Administration or his authorized representative.

(b) "Extra-terrestrially exposed" means the state of condition of any person, property, animal or other form of life or matter whatever, who or which has:

(1) Touched directly or come within the atmospheric envelope or any other celestial body; or

190

(2) Touched directly or been in close proximity to (or been exposed indirectly to) any person, property, animal or other form of life or matter who or which has been extra-terrestrially exposed by virtue of paragraph (b)(1) of this section.

For example, if person or thing "A" touches the surface of the Moon, and on "A's" return to Earth, "B" touches "A" and, subsequently, "C" touches "B", all of these - "A" through "C" inclusive - would be extra-terrestrially exposed ("A" and "B" directly; "C" indirectly).

(c) "Quarantine" means the detention, examination and decontamination of any persons, property, animal or other form of life or matter whatever that is extra-terrestrially exposed, and includes the apprehension or seizure of such person, property, animal or other form of life or matter whatever.

(d) "Quarantine period" means a period of consecutive calendar days as may be established in accordance with 1211.104 (a).

(a) Administrative actions. The Administrator or his designee shall in his discretion:

(1) Determine the beginning and duration of a quarantine period with respect to any space mission; the quarantine period as it applies to various life forms will be announced.

(2) Designate in writing quarantine officers to exercise quarantine authority.

(3) Determine that a particular person, property, animal, or other form of life or matter whatever is extra- terrestrially exposed and quarantine such person, property, animal, or other form of life or matter whatever. The quarantine may be based only on a determination, with or without the benefit of a hearing, that there is probable cause to believe that such person, property, animal or other form of life or matter whatever is extra- terrestrially exposed.

(4) Determine within the United States or within vessels or vehicles of the United States the place, boundaries, and rules of operation of necessary quarantine stations.

(5) Provide for guard services by contract or otherwise, as many be necessary, to maintain security and inviolability of quarantine stations and quarantined persons, property, animals or other form of life or matter whatever.

(6) Provide for the subsistence, health and welfare of persons quarantined under the provisions of this part.

(7) Hold such hearings at such times, in such manner and for such purposes as may be desirable or necessary under this part, including hearings for the purpose of creating a record for use in making any determination under this part for the purpose of reviewing any such determination.

(b) (3) During any period of announced quarantine, no person shall enter or depart from the limits of the quarantine station without permission of the cognizant NASA officer. During such period, the posted perimeter of a quarantine station shall be secured by armed guard.

(b) (4) Any person who enters the limits of any quarantine station during the quarantine period shall be deemed to have consented to the quarantine of his person if it is determined that he is or has become extra-terrestrially exposed.

(b) (5) At the earliest practicable time, each person who is quarantined by NASA shall be given a reasonable opportunity to communicate by telephone with legal counsel or other persons of his choice.

1211.107 Court or other process

(a) NASA officers and employees are prohibited from discharging from the limits of a quarantine station any quarantined person, property, animal or other form of life or matter whatever during order or other request, order or demand an announced quarantine period in compliance with a subpoena, show cause or any court or other authority without the prior approval of the General Counsel and the Administrator.

(b) Where approval to discharge a quarantined person, property, animal or other form of life or matter whatever in compliance with such a request, order or demand of any court or other authority is not given, the person to whom it is directed shall, if possible, appear in court or before the other authority and respectfully state his inability to comply, relying for his action on this

1211.108 Violations

Whoever willfully violates, attempts to violate, or conspires to violate any provision of this part or any regulation or order issued under this part or who enters or departs from the limits of a quarantine station in disregard of the quarantine rules or regulations or without permission of the NASA quarantine officer shall be fined not more that $5,000 or imprisoned not more than 1 year, or both.

APPENDIX E: MY COMMENTS ON THE DOCUMENT *RESEARCH FINDINGS ON CHIHUAHUA DISK CRASH* BY ELAINE DOUGLASS (7/10/2006)

This document appears to have originated from a group of government employees lacking a need-to-know about ET-related government activities, but who are attempting to find out what is going on—much as described by Howard Blum in his book *Out There*. The document is fact-packed, and so we see that the group of government employees, the "Deneb team," was not shut out, but in fact succeeded in developing considerable information about an ET-related event even though they did not have a need to know.

This suggests a significant degree of awareness among government personnel of the reality of UFOs, as well as considerable sharing of information on ET-related government activities among government persons. And not just a passive interest, but in some quarters—the "Deneb team" for example—there is a determined effort to amass such information. What is the reason for this determined effort? I wonder, and what is the use to which these determined persons put the information they gather?

People who work for the government, especially in national security agencies, are no less likely than are we civilian ufo researchers to recognize the reality of UFOs. Moreover, they are often in a much better position to recognize traces of the cover-up, to infer, that is, the existence of a cover up, than civilian researchers are, as discussed in Bruce Maccabee's article "Hiding the Hardware." Or, to go beyond mere inference and learn of undeniably ET-related events, such as the 1974 Chihuahua crash. Undoubtedly, some are transfixed by the importance of the ET matter and consumed by curiosity about it, as we are, but they cannot join civilian ufo organizations, research cases, and write articles as we do. The frustration of such individuals can be imagined, so what do they do?

What the document suggests they do is form quiet little unofficial study groups whose members set about discretely gathering information about ET-related government activities. Let's call that the A model. Alternatively, a B model is where the study group is not completely unofficial, but is instead semi-official. More about that below.

First, the author of the document, "JS," what kind of sources did he or she have access to? Very significantly, the author had access to written reports. This is explicitly mentioned in para. 20. Also, in para. 19, the manner of presentation of information suggests to me the information was drawn from a written document. Also para. 23, which says, "No mention is made of the occupants of the civilian aircraft." This sounds like the information came from a written source, providing no one for the author to interrogate and ask, 'What was done with the bodies from the civilian aircraft?'

The author seems to have had oral conversations regarding the event. In para. 18, it says "one unconfirmed report . . ." and "another [unconfirmed report]. . ." People are speculating, and that suggests conversations between the author and others, though speculations can be embodied in written reports.

Para. 11 refers to an "eye witness." Surely this witness is an individual working or stationed at the time at Ft. Bliss who was not involved in the recovery operation and who watched from afar as the recovery team assembled. Perhaps the witness was a woman, because she is a good observer but she does not recognize helicopters by model name, and it seems like most men at Ft. Bliss would.

The document is a strictly factual recitation, and contains no hint of the context in which the author was operating. Nonetheless, there is also no hint the author felt any apprehension of getting found out and reprimanded as he went about gathering classified information which he had no need to know. More to the contrary, if there is any sense of context it is that numbers of persons within the government cooperate in providing each other with ET-related information none of them are supposed to have, or at least some of them are not supposed to have. Furthermore, the designation "FILE UFO3263" at the top of the document indicates first that the term "ufo" is used in government circles, contrary to what some have claimed. And second that the document was to be added to or was already part of a large collection of carefully catalogued "UFO" documents.

What might be the disposition of information gathered on a basis—assume now model A in which the Deneb team is just a group of friends-- such as I have described above? That is problematic, isn't it? The normal human tendency, upon gathering information, is to publish it. That outlet denied, presumably the Deneb team members must content themselves by simply consuming the information among themselves. Perhaps a modest equivalent to "publishing" would be to share the information over time and occasionally with other government employees.

If such "quiet little unofficial study groups" exist throughout the national security agencies, and that would not surprise me, why do we civilian researchers not hear from them more often? It is not because their identities would be compromised, since the information could be anonymously leaked, as this document was. I imagine we do not hear from them more often because they hold an implicit belief that they have a right to UFO/ET information, but we, members of the public, do not. Even though they are not in the loop, they are engaged in the national security function and they will at least hold such information amongst themselves, while we civilian researchers will trumpet it to the masses.

The B model as to why this information was acquired and what use it might be put to, is not radically different from the A model. In the B model, the Deneb team is not so unofficial as posited in the A model. In the B model, the Deneb team was assembled and tasked by a high official, someone who commands a staff and has a budget and authority to deploy resources at his or her discretion. In the B model, the Deneb team is not operating in their "spare time," but is carrying out their inquiries on salary.

Any high official acquainted with the reality of the ET presence and who knows a secret bureaucracy within the larger bureaucracy operates in response to this presence, knows that here is a matter of surpassing importance. Any high official with this awareness but not in the loop on the ET matter, would know themselves to be at a disadvantage and might well seek to rectify that disadvantage by gathering information.

Let's say a high official is spending money and staff time to gather ET information, and has amassed at least one file cabinet full of documents. What does the high official do with this information? True, he or she simply feels better, not in the dark like a child. But, is that enough to justify the time and expenditure?

Let's say the high official is motivated by some blend of deep concern about the ET matter combined with a desire to gain career advantage. That would make the official like we UFO researchers, who have deep concern about the ET matter and we also want to get invited to speak at conferences and see our byline on published articles. How would the high official use the information to gain career advantage? It's hard to say, isn't it? Just speculating, perhaps the high official says to him or herself: Why do some other people prevail in the decision-making arena, and why do they get bigger budgets than I do when their overt arguments and their overt programs cannot be justified?

If we're talking weapons systems, examples might be why does DOD continue to invest in nuclear attack submarines when there aren't any Soviet subs in the water anymore? Or why does DOD have an SDI program when for years it was profoundly well-established doctrine that efforts to shoot ballistic missiles out of the sky are a fool's errand? If the high official has a file cabinet full of ufo documents, the information in that cabinet might inform the official what lies behind some of these bureaucratic manifestations. Mine are no doubt crude characterizations of bureaucratic motivation, but the fact remains that if we use model B, we would like to know what is the career advantage our high official gains by amassing ufo/ET information?

One thing is certain. Whether the Deneb team operated unofficially, or semi-officially, the persons involved in the Deneb team effort were not in the loop, they were not part of the cover-up. So what we are seeing is an example of parts of the government spying on other parts of the government.

Another thing seems apparent, and that is that the "Report on the Chihuahua Disk Crash" was stolen from whoever controlled the document. It seems the document was stolen, retyped, and the words "[report is abruptly interrupted at this point]" were added at the end as a note of explanation to whomever outside the government the document would reach. I suspect the document was stolen because whoever mailed the document out did not have access to the whole document. That means the document was not leaked by any member of the "Deneb team."

Let me turn now to a different subject.

While I was MUFON state director Washington DC, and well before I received the Denab team document in the mail, I was contacted by an individual recently discharged from the military who told me something of interest indirectly related to the Mexican disk crash. The individual told me that while he was in the military he served with a unit whose function was to go inside foreign countries, perform some task and get out quickly without the government of the foreign country knowing the unit had been there.

The man who contacted me, and I met him on one occasion in a coffee shop in DC, was in his late 30s. He showed me his military records, which were in plastic sleeves in a 3-ring binder. He said that the unit he served with was stationed in the United States and was not unique. That is, that there are several such teams in readiness at all times.

He did not describe the range of types of missions teams such as he served in performed, nor did he say explicitly that his team had been on any UFO-related missions, but somehow he made it plain that recovering ET physical evidence was one of types of missions that his team and other teams like it were prepared to undertake and had undertaken. I recall him saying that he and his fellow servicemen used to stay up late at night talking about UFOs and ET and wondering what was their ultimate significance.

I recall him telling me some data about the speed and range of the vehicles the teams used to get around and I figured out the maximum time they could be gone and he was impressed. Or perhaps it was that he told me the time and the range and I figured the speed. I am not sure what the data parameters were other than he told me two parameters and I computed the third, and I recall he raised his eyebrows and said yes that's correct.

He said that when men return from these missions they are so tense and wound up—from lack of sleep, perhaps unable to have had bowel movements, perhaps taking drugs—that if you even speak to them, much less hassle them, they would punch you out. They are irrational on return due to stress. I note para. 17 of the document relates that the US truck convoy which received the disk from a helicopter at 2:30 am in western Texas "continued non-stop using back roads" until it reached Atlanta. Some of the personnel who had been in Mexico joined the truck convoy, and the convoy personnel must have been en route for some time prior to the rendezvous. All these men were on the job many hours prior to the rendezvous and would be for all the hours until Atlanta, possibly more. I don't know if "non-stop" means they didn't stop even for bathroom breaks, but it probably does mean they weren't lolling around for long lunches at coffee shops. This is consistent with the high stress assignments my informant described.

The one thing my informant told me I will never forget—he said his team had standing orders not to return any bodies. On the face of it this would have to include human or ET bodies. What this statement meant to me is that the US government has so many alien bodies they don't need any more.

After my meeting with the informant, which lasted perhaps an hour, I several times sent him mail in an effort to arrange a second meeting, but to no avail. He told me he has a wife and children and had entered college in Maryland. My impression was that in retrospect, in his own mind, he was appalled he had contacted and he saw no reason for further contact, which could jeopardize his post-discharge benefits (probably college assistance) or worse.

At present I do not have his name, address and any notes I may have made at hand. It seems unlikely I discarded this information, but I do not know where in my files the information may be. However, finding it is an incentive to me to clean and reorganize my files, something I intend to do in the near future. On the other hand, it is highly unlikely his address remains the same, although if I had his name perhaps he could be located somewhere in the United States.

My contact with this individual occurred several years prior to my receipt of "Research Findings on the C Disk Crash," and I see no connection between that contact and the document.

It should be noted that the person who wrote the Denab team document did not know of the existence of clandestine rapid response teams such as described by my informant. Para. 9 of the document says, ". . . forming a recovery team. The speed with which this team . . . was assembled suggests this was either a well-rehearsed exercise or one that had been performed prior to this event." My informant's information suggests that such teams are standing teams ready at all times to perform missions such as the disk recovery in Mexico.

BIBLIOGRAPHY

"1948 7/8 July. 2.30pm Laredo/30mi Inside Mexico." *Center for the Study of Extraterrestrial Intelligence*. 30 Dec. 2005 <http://www.cseti.org/crashes/022.html>.

"23 December 4, 1952 2046-2053L UM 8 Mi. SW, Laredo, Texas." *National Aviation Reporting Center on Anomalous Phenomena*. 29 Jan. 2006 <http://www.narcap.org>.

"60. Location Near Del Rio, Mexico." *1950 Humanoid Sighting Reports*. 21 Jan. 2006 <http://ufoinfo.com>.

"7-7-48 Laredo." *UFO Crash and Alien Recoveries*. 28 Jan. 2006 <http://www.burlingtonnews.net/ufocrashes.html>.

"Air Force Order on 'Saucers' Cited." *The New York Times* 28 Feb. 1960: 30. *ProQuest*. Historical Newspapers. 12 Feb. 2006.

"Air Force Orders Jet Pilots to Shoot Down Flying Saucers If They Refuse to Land." *Post-Intelligencer* (Seattle, WA) 29 July 1952: 1.

Allen, Don. "Re: AIR #1 Report - 1/10." *Skeptic Tank Text Archive File*. Jan. 2006 <http://www.skepticfiles.org/index.htm>.

"Athena Missile Goes Awry, Falls in Mexico." *Los Angeles Times*. 12 July 1970: 4. *ProQuest*. Historical Newspapers. 2 June 2006.

"Athena Tests Said Suspended." *Washington Post*. 30 July 1970: A14. *ProQuest*. Historical Newspapers. 2 June 2006.

Auldbridge, Larry. "Jets on 24-Hour Alert To Shoot Down 'Saucers'." *San Francisco Examiner*. 29 July 1952.

Baeza, Javier Nieto. Personal Interview. 28 Oct. 2006.

Baeza, Salome. Personal Interview. 4 Jan. 2007.

Baldwin, Hanson W. "Scientists Track Wild V-2 Rocket As Crowds Visit Crater in Juarez." *New York Times*. 31 May 1947: 14. *ProQuest*. Historical Newspapers. 2 June 2006.

Baldwin, Hanson W. "Wild V-2 Rocket 'Invades' Mexico; Backtracks in a White Sands Test." *New York Times*. 30 May 1947: 1. *ProQuest*. Historical Newspapers. 2 June 2006.

Berliner, Don, and Stanton T. Friedman. *Crash At Corona: the U.S. Military Retrieval and Cover-Up of a UFO*. New York:

Marlowe & Company, 1992.

Berlitz, Charles, and William L. Moore. *The Roswell Incident.* Berkeley Books: New York, 1980.

Booth, B J. "1974 Aug 25 - Coyame, Chihuahua, Mexico-Disk Crashes." *UFO Casebook.* 20 Dec. 2005 <http://www.ufocasebook.com>.

Booth, B J. "Coyame." Email to the authors. 17 Jun. 2006.

Broad, William J. "Administration Researches Laser Weapon." *New York Times.* 3 May 2006. <www.nytimes.com>

Bryant, John. Personal Interview. 5 Jan. 2007.

Bryant, Soledad. Personal Interview. 4 Jan. 2007.

Carlotto, Mark J. "Digital Video Analysis of Anomalous Space Objects." *Journal of Scientific Exploration.* Vol. 9, No. 1, 1995. 45-63.

Cervantes, Filemon. Personal Interview. 3 Jan. 2007.

"Chihuahua Disk Crash, The." *Center for the Study of Extraterrestrial Intelligence.* 20 Dec. 2005 <http://www.cseti.org/crashes/050.htm>.

Clark, Jerome. *The UFO Book.* Detroit: Visible Ink Press, 1998.

Clark, Jerome, and Nancy Pear. *Strange & Unexplained Happenings: When Nature Breaks the Rules of Science.* Vol. 1. New York: UXL, 1995.

Cohen, Daniel. *The Great Airship Mystery: a UFO of the 1890s.* New York: Dodd, Mead & Company, 1981.

"Colección Fenómenos Extraños." *Mundo Paranormal.* 20 Apr. 2006 < http://www.mundoparanormal.com>.

Colloff, Pamela. "1948: Laredo, Texas (Close Encounters of the Lone Star Kind)." *Texas Monthly.* 28 Jan. 2006 <http://www.texasmonthly.com/ranch/ufo/laredo.php>.

Colloff, Pamela. "Close Encounters of the Lone Star Kind." *Texas Monthly.* 28 Jan. 2006 <http://www.texasmonthly.com/ranch/ufo>.

"Corona." *National Reconnaissance Office.* United States National Reconnaissance Office. 27 Jan. 2006 <http://www.nro.gov/>.

Corrales, Scott. "Beyond Reality: Mexico's Zone of Silence." *Strange Mag.* 30 Dec. 2005 <http://www.strangemag.com>.

"Coyame Del Sotol." *Enciclopedia De Los Municipios De Mexico.* 27 Dec. 2005 <http://www.e-local.gob.mx>.

Deuley, Tom. "Del Rio 1950." Email to the authors. 4 Apr. 2006.

"Discover AWOL Rocket Caused A-Bomb Scare." *Chicago Daily Tribune.* 31 May 1947: 9. *ProQuest.* Historical Newspapers. 2 June 2006.

Dittman, Geoff. "An Examination Into Close Encounters Involving Death, Injury, or Healing of the Witness." <http://www.geocities.com/Area51/Rampart/2653/>

Dobbs, Michael. "Into Thin Air." *The Washington Post* 26 Oct. 2003, sec. W: 4.

"Documents Dated 1948-1959." *Majestic Documents: Evidence We are Not Alone.* Jan. 2006 <http://www.majesticdocuments.com>.

Dolan, Richard M. "UFO Secrecy and the Death of the Republic." *Through the Keyhole.* 28 Feb. 2005. 24 Jan. 2006 <http://keyholepublishing.com>.

Douglass, Elaine. "My Comments On the Document *Research Findings on Chihuahua Disk Crash.*" Email to the authors. 10 July 2006.

Eckles, Jim. "The Athena That Got Away." *White Sands Missile Range.* United States Army. 2 June 2006 <http://www.wsmr.army.mil/>.

"El Caso Coyame: Se precipito un OVNI en territorio mexicano en 1974?" *Los Grandes Misterios Del Trecer Milenio, No.5.* Jaime Maussan Productions. 2006.

"El Paso Sees Flying Bomb." *Los Angeles Times* 13 Oct. 1947: 1. *ProQuest.* Historical Newspapers. 2 June 2006.

"Electronic Reading Room." *Central Intelligence Agency Freedom of Information Act Documents.* Central Intelligence Agency. Jan. 2006 <http://www.foia.cia.gov>.

"Errant Army Missile Takes Mexican Trip." *Chicago Tribune.* 13 Sept. 1967: C14. *ProQuest.* Historical Newspapers. 2 June 2006.

"Errant Missile Thought Found." *Los Angeles Times.* 20 Sept. 1967: 4. *ProQuest.* Historical Newspapers. 2 June 2006.

"Exhibits: End of a War; Beginning of a Laboratory, Z Division, 1945-1949." *Sandia History Program & Corporate Archives.* 11 Oct. 2004. Sandia National Laboratories. 24 Jan. 2006 <http://www.sandia.gov/recordsmgmt/zdiv.html>.

"Flaming Mystery Startles Texans, Crosses Border." *Associated Press.* 12 Oct. 1947.

"Flying Saucer Crash With Midget Told." *Los Angeles Times* 10 Mar. 1950: 2. *ProQuest.* Historical Newspapers. 12 Mar. 2006.

"Flying Saucer, Midget Pilot Reported Landing in Mexico." *Washington Times-Herald* 10 Mar. 1950.

"Ford UFO Talk." *The Presidents UFO Web Site.* 30 Jan. 2006 <http://www.presidentialufo.com/ufotalk.htm>.

Fowler, Raymond E. *Casebook of a UFO Investigator.* Englewood Cliffs, NJ: Prentice-Hall, Inc., 1981. 196-208.

Friedman, Stanton T. *Top Secret / Majic.* New York: Marlowe & Company, 1996.

Friedman, Stanton T. "UFOs No Security Threat?" *MUFON UFO Journal.* June 2005. 20-21.

Garwood, Darrell. "Jets Told to Shoot Down Flying Discs." *Herald-News.* (Fall River, MA) 29 July 1952: 1.

González, Jorge A. Almeida. "Rancho El Murciélago." Emails to the authors. July 2006.

Gross, Loren E. *UFOs: A History, Volume 5: January-March, 1950.* Fremont, California. 1983.

Haines, Gerald K. "CIA's Role in the Study of UFOs, 1947-1990." *Central Intelligence Agency Unclassified Documents.* 1 Nov. 1997. Central Intelligence Agency. 12 Feb. 2006 <http://www.cia.gov/csi/studies/97unclass/ufo.html>.

Haines, Gerald. "The CIA's Role in the Study of UFOs, 1947-90." *CIA Freedom of Information Archives.* 18 Jan. 2006 <http://www.foia.cia.gov>.

Hall, Richard. *The UFO Evidence, Volume 2: A Thirty Year Report.* Lanham, MD: Scarecrow Press, 2001. 133.

Handbook of Texas Online, The. Texas State Historical Association. Jan. 2006 <http://www.tsha.utexas.edu/handbook/online/>.

Howe, Linda Moulton. *Secret Radar Stations in New Mexico, Parts 1 & 2.* 2000 <http://www.earthfiles.com>.

"Images and Photos on-Line." *U.S. Army Medical Department & School Portal.* United States Army. 24 Jan. 2006 <http://www.cs.armedd.army.mil/history/pics.html>.

"James Webb and the December 6, 1950 UFO Alert." *The*

Presidents UFO Web Site. 21 Jan. 2006
  <http://www.presidentialufo.com/ufo_alert.htm>.
Kaus, Andrea. "The Zone of Silence." *Planeta World Guide*. 1992.
  31 July 2006 < http://www.planeta.com/>.
Kimball, Paul. "Oh Canada - Wilbert Smith & UFOs." *The Other
  Side of Truth*. 2 Mar. 2005. 30 Jan. 2006
  <http://redstarfilms.blogspot.com>.
Kinney, Terry. "Man Says He Has Proof Aliens Have Visited U.S."
  UFO Evidence. 29 Apr. 1980. 29 Jan. 2006
  <http://www.ufoevidence.org>.
Kissner, J. Andrew. *Peculiar Phenomenon: Early United States
  Efforts to Collect and Analyze Flying Discs*. 1994
  <http://www.earthfiles.com>.
Kramer, William M. and Charles Bahme. *Fire Officer's Guide to
  Disaster Control*. Saddle Brook, NJ: Fire Engineering Books
  & Videos, 1992.
Kruger, Hans. *Radiation-Neutralization of Stored Biological
  Warfare Agents with Low-Yield Nuclear Warheads*. U.S.
  Dept. of Energy Lawrence Livermore National Laboratory.
  Springfield, VA: U.S. Department of Energy, 2000.
"Laredo Crash." *Alien Conspiracy*. 28 Jan. 2006
  <http://members.tripod.com/~AlienConspiracy/crashes/
  laredo.htm>.
"Laredo Texas - 3 November 1952." *Project Blue Book Archive*. 3
  Nov. 1952. 28 Jan. 2006 <http://www.bluebookarchive.org>.
Maccabee, Bruce. "Dec 1950 Crash & Willingham." *UFO Updates*.
  19 Jan. 2001. 25 Jan. 2006
  <http://www.virtuallystrange.net/ufo/updates/2001/jan/m20-
  003.shtml>.
Maccabee, Bruce. "Del Rio 1950." Email to the authors. 27 Jan.
  2006.
Maccabee, Bruce. "Immediate Saucer Alert! the Mystery of
  December 6, 1950." *National Investigations Committee on
  Aerial Phenomena*. 21 Jan. 2006
  <http://www.nicap.org/reports/rena4.htm>.
Maccabee, Bruce. "Radar Inspired National Alert." *National
  Investigations Committee on Aerial Phenomena*. 22 Jan.
  2006 <http://www.nicap.org/reports/rina2.htm>.

"Majestic 12." *Federal Bureau of Investigation Freedom of Information Privacy Act*. Federal Bureau of Investigation. 12 Feb. 2006 <http://foia.fbi.gov/foiaindex/majestic.htm>.

Maldonado, Carlos, and Patricio Maldonado. "La Fascinante Zona Del Silencio." *Mexico Desconocido*. Apr. 1996. 30 Dec. 2005 <http://www.mexicodesconocido.com.mx>.

Marrs, Jim. *Alien Agenda: Investigating the Extraterrestrial Presence Among Us*. New York: Harper Paperbacks, 1997.

"Marshall Blamed For UFO Coverup" *Pittsburgh Tribune-Review* 12 February 2006. 4 May 2006 <http://www.pittsburghlive.com/>.

McAndrew, James. "Report on Project Mogul: Synopsis of Balloon Research Findings." *Muller's Group - Lawrence Berkeley Laboratory*. 21 Sept. 1995. United States Air Force. 14 Feb. 2006 <http://muller.lbl.gov>.

"Mexicans Seek Lost U.S. Missile." *Washington Post*. 14 July 1970: A3. *ProQuest*. Historical Newspapers. 2 June 2006.

"Mexico Reports Missile." *New York Times* 13 Oct. 1947: 15. *ProQuest*. Historical Newspapers. 2 June 2006.

"Mexico's Roswell." *UFO Files*. History Channel. Time-Warner Cable, Harlingen, TX. 12 Dec. 2005.

"Military Bases Suspected of UFO Activity." *Alien Astronomer*. 13 Jan. 2006 <http://www.geocities.com/Area51/Shadowlands/6583/>.

"Mysterious Mexican Blast Is Reported." *Washington Post*. 13 Oct. 1947: 3. *ProQuest*. Historical Newspapers. 2 June 2006.

"Mystery Blast." *Chicago Daily Tribune*. 13 Oct. 1947: 8. *ProQuest*. Historical Newspapers. 2 June 2006.

"Nation Urged Not to Shoot at 'Saucers.'" *Los Angeles Times* 30 July 1952: 1. *ProQuest*. Historical Newspapers. 24 July 2006.

"NARA-PBB90-928." *Project Blue Book Archive*. 26 Sept. 1960. 21 Jan. 2006 <http://www.bluebookarchive.org>.

Nelson, Mike. "The Desert - the Zone of Silence." *Mexico Mike's Mexico*. 30 Dec. 2005 <http://www.mexicomike.com/stories/zone.htm>.

"No Title." *The Washington Post* 7 Dec. 1950: 2. *ProQuest*. Historical Newspapers. 25 Jan. 2006.

Ogulnick, Richard. "La Zona Del Silencio." 30 Dec. 2005
    <http://www.geocities.com/Athens/5484/4-zona.htm>.
Olson, Alexandra. "Puerto Rico Farming Town to Build UFO
    Landing Strip." *USA Today Online.* 28 Sept. 2005. 23 June
    2006. <http://www.usatoday.com>.
"Parts of Stray Missile Found." *New York Times.* 24 Sept. 1967: 58.
    ProQuest. Historical Newspapers. 2 June 2006.
Pearson, Drew. "Air Force Admission on Saucers." *Washington
    Post.* 29 July 1952: 29. *ProQuest.* Historical Newspapers. 24
    July 2006.
"Perry-Castañeda Library Texas Maps." *The University of Texas At
    Austin General Libraries.* The University of Texas at Austin.
    <http://www.lib.utexas.edu/maps/texas.html>.
"Piper P-24 Paced By Three Flying Discs, 1975." *Casebook: Radar
    Visual Cases.* 19 Apr. 2006
    <http://ufologie.net/htm/montiel75.htm>.
"Project 1947: A Ghost Rocket Chronology." *Project 1947.* Sign
    Historical Group. <http://www.project1947.com>.
Ramirez, Giovanna M. "Mexican Roswell." Email to the authors. 3
    Feb. 2006.
Randle, Kevin D., and Donald R. Schmitt. *The Truth About the UFO
    Crash At Roswell.* New York: Avon Books, 1994.
Randle, Kevin D., and Donald R. Schmitt. *UFO Crash At Roswell.*
    New York: Avon Books, 1991. 248-250.
Randle, Kevin D., and Russ Estes. *Spaceships of the Visitors: an
    Illustrated Guide to Alien Spacecraft.* New York: Simon &
    Schuster, 2000.
Randle, Kevin D. *Case MJ-12: the True Story Behind the
    Government's UFO Conspiracies.* New York: HarperTorch,
    2002.
Randle, Kevin D. *Conspiracy of Silence.* New York: Avon Books,
    1997.
Randle, Kevin D. *A History of UFO Crashes.* New York: Avon
    Books, 1995.
Randle, Kevin D. *Invasion Washington: UFOs Over the Capitol.*
    New York: HarperTorch, 2001.
Randles, Jenny, and Peter Hough. *The Complete Book of UFOs.*
    New York: Sterling Company, 1994.

"Regret Expressed to Mexico." *New York Times.* 31 May 1947: 14. *ProQuest.* Historical Newspapers. 2 June 2006.

Ritchie, David. *The Definitive Guide to Unidentified Flying Objects and Related Phenomena.* New York: Facts on File, 1994. 56.

Rivera Altamirano, Gilberto E. "Caso Coyame." *Expediente X Casos Locales.* Grupo de Investigación de Fenómenos Aeroespaciales (GIFAE). 14 July 2006 <http://espanol.geocities.com/gifae/xfiles13.htm>.

"Robert A. Lovett." *SecDef Histories.* United States Department of Defense. 23 Jan. 2006 <http://www.defenselink.mil/>.

Rojas, Carlos Alberto Guzman, and Francisco Dominguez de la Rosa. "Pilot Says Plane Was Controlled by UFOs." *MUFON UFO Journal.* Jan. 2003. 3-5.

Rojas, Carlos Alberto Guzman, and Francisco Dominguez de la Rosa. "Mexican Pilot Relates Possible MIB Contacts Following Encounter." *MUFON UFO Journal.* Feb. 2003. 5-7.

"Roper Poll: UFOs & Extraterrestrial Life." *The Sci Fi Channel.* 12 Feb. 2006 <http://www.scifi.com/ufo/roper/>.

"Roswell Teletype." *Federal Bureau of Investigation Freedom of Information Privacy Act.* 8 July 1947. Federal Bureau of Investigation. 14 Feb. 2006 <http://foia.fbi.gov/foiaindex/roswell.htm>.

"Rocket Fired in U.S. Blows Up in Mexico." *Chicago Daily Tribune.* 30 May 1947: 1. *ProQuest.* Historical Newspapers. 2 June 2006.

Schaffner, Ron. "Tomato Man Revisited." *Anomoly Research Commentary.* 29 Jan. 006 <http://home.fuse.net/arcsite/tomato.htm>.

Schoenmann, Joe. "Believe!" *Las Vegas Weekly* 27 Nov. 2003. 27 Jan. 2006 <http://www.lasvegasweekly.com>.

Scully, Frank. *Behind the Flying Saucers.* Popular Library, 1951.

"Searchers Fail to Find Rocket." *New York Times.* 14 Sept. 1967: 60. *ProQuest.* Historical Newspapers. 2 June 2006.

Snell, Scott. "Investigation Shows No Link Between Saucer Crash Tale and 1950 UFO Report." *Skeptical Eye* 1999. 2 Apr. 2006 <http://www.ncas.org/eyes/SE-11.4.pdf>.

Sobel, Dava. "The Truth About Roswell - Alleged Crash of a UFO Near Roswell, NM, on Jun 25, 1947." *Omni* Fall 1995.

FindArticles. LookSmart. 27 Jan. 2006.

Stacy, Dennis. "Crash At El Indio - Alleged UFO Crash in Mexico." *Omni* Mar. 1995. *FindArticles.* 22 June 2006.

Steinman, William S., and Wendelle C. Stevens. *UFO Crash At Aztec: A Well Kept Secret.* Tucson: America West Distributors, 1986.

Stringfield, Leonard H. *UFO Crash/Retrievals, Status Reports I-VII.* 1978-1984.

Story, Ronald D., ed. *The Encyclopedia of UFOs.* Garden City, NY: Dolphin Books, 1980.

Sutton, Paul. "Low-Yield Nuclear Weapon." Email to the authors. 16 Jan. 2006.

"Tale of Saucer – and Midget Pilot." *Chicago Daily Tribune* 10 Mar. 1950: 1. *ProQuest.* Historical Newspapers. 12 Mar. 2006.

"Tesla, At 78, Bares New 'Death-Beam.'" *New York Times.* 11 July 1934: 18. *ProQuest.* Historical Newspapers. 23 June 2006.

"Tomato Man Photographs of Alien Body From Laredo, Texas Crash." *UFO Evidence.* 28 Jan. 2006 <http://ufoevidence.org/cases/case378.htm>.

"UFO Crash in Laredo, Texas, USA 1948." *UFOs At Close Sight.* 9 Feb. 2001. 28 Jan. 2006 <http://ufologie.net/htm/laredo48.htm>.

"UFO Roundup: Volume 10, Number 7." *UFOInfo.* 16 Feb. 2005. 20 Apr. 2006. <http://www.ufoinfo.com/roundup/v10/rnd1007.shtml>.

"UFO Updates." *VSN - the Virtually Strange Network.* Jan. 2006 <http://www.virtuallystrange.net/ufo/updates/2000/dec/m13-019.shtml>.

"UFO Case Report: UFOs Escort Mexican Aircraft." *UFO Evidence.* 19 Apr. 2006 <http://ufoevidence.org/cases/case311.htm>.

"Unarmed Pershing Missile Strays Into Mexico." *New York Times.* 13 Sept. 1967: 24. *ProQuest.* Historical Newspapers. 2 June 2006.

"Unidentified Flying Objects." *Federal Bureau of Investigation Freedom of Information Privacy Act.* Federal Bureau of Investigation. Jan. 2006

<http://foia.fbi.gov/foiaindex/ufo.htm>.

"Unidentified Flying Objects Research Guide." *U.S. Naval Historical Center*. 7 Mar. 2002. United State Navy. Feb. 2006 <http://www.history.navy.mil/faqs/faq29-1.htm>.

Uriarte, Ruben. Miscellaneous emails to Noe Torres. 2006.

USAF Museum. United States Air Force. Jan. 2006 <http://www.wpafb.af.mil/museum>.

"U.S. Air Force Comes to Town, The." *Del Rio Chamber of Commerce*. 22 Jan. 2006 <http://www.drchamber.com/live/history/usaf.php>.

Valeriano, Leandro. Personal Interview. 5 Jan. 2007.

Venegas, Pedro Leyva. Personal Interview. 4 Jan. 2007.

Von Daniken, Erich. *Chariots of the Gods*. New York: Berkley Books, 1999.

"Wild V-2 Rocket Blast Shakes El Paso Region." *Los Angeles Times.* 30 May 1947: 1. *ProQuest*. Historical Newspapers. 2 June 2006.

Wood, Ryan S. "Dr. Robert Dunglison Evans." *Majestic Documents.Com: Evidence We are Not Alone*. 1 Apr. 2006 <http://www.majesticdocuments.com/personnel/evans.php>.

Wood, Ryan S. *Majic Eyes Only: Earth's Encounters with Extraterrestrial Technology*. Broomfield, CO: Wood Enterprises, 2005. 95-184.

"World Air Forces: Mexico." *Aeroflight*. 17 Jan. 2001. 21 Jan. 2006 <http://www.aeroflight.co.uk/index.html>.

York, Warren. "UFO Update." *Internet Sacred Text Archive*. 26 Dec. 2005 <http://www.sacred-texts.com/ufo/ufochey1.htm>.

"Zona De Silencio: Paralelo 27." *Kodak InCamera*. 30 Dec. 2005 <http://www.kodak.com>.

Deneb Report, the, 63, 64, 65,
66, 67, 68, 69, 70, 82, 89,
92, 98, 118, 160, 178, 194,
195, 196, 197
Desden Codex (Mexico), 163,
164
Douglass, Elaine, UFO
researcher, 26, 41, 63, 64,
65, 66, 67, 68, 69, 194
Ehman, Dr. Jerry R., 5
Eisenhower Briefing
Document (EBD), 141,
142, 143, 186
El Cuervo, Chihuhua, Mexico,
84, 151, 152
El Indio, TX, 188
El Llano, 1, 2, 3, 17, 19, 37,
74, 76, 85, 87, 92, 93, 94,
95, 105, 107, 108
El Paso, TX, 2, 13, 14, 21, 22,
24, 26, 28, 31, 35, 37, 51,
60, 110, 145, 146, 147, 149,
179
Ellington AFB, Houston, TX,
10, 51
Fabens, TX, 148
Fire Officer's Guide to
Disaster Control, 117, 118
*Ford, Gerald R., U.S.
President*, 8, 25
Fort Bliss Army Base, TX, 22,
23, 24, 26, 31, 32, 33, 34,
35, 37, 39, 44, 51, 65, 92,
145, 147, 148, 149, 180,
195
González Almeida, Jorge A.,
19, 20, 39, 74, 76, 81, 82
Groom Lake, NV, 51

Hillenkoetter, Roscoe H., CIA
Director, 6, 186
Iztaccihuatl volcano, 128, 129
Keyhole spy satellite, 22, 30
Kingsville, TX, 10
Kirtland AFB, NM, 51
Kissner, J. Andy, 146, 147
Lackland AFB, San Antonio,
TX, 10
Laughlin AFB, Del Rio, TX,
13
Lennon, John, 8
Maccabee, Bruce, UFO
researcher, 194
Majestic 12 (MJ-12)
documents, 120, 121
Marfa, TX, 15, 157, 158, 160
Maussan, Jaime, UFO
researcher, 61, 78, 79
Maya (Mexico), 163, 164
Mexico City, Mexico, 21, 23,
59, 60, 83, 124, 125, 126,
127, 128, 129, 130, 131,
132, 138, 139, 140, 141,
147, 148, 149, 163, 165,
167, 179
NASA, U.S. Space Agency, 7,
22, 41, 129, 133, 144, 145,
190, 192, 193
Olmecs of Mexico, 163
Panspermia, 118, 120
Pershing missile crash in
Mexico, 84, 149, 150, 151,
152
Popocatépetl volcano, 128,
129, 161, 165
Presidio, TX, 15, 92, 180

211

Printed in the United States
107281LV00004B/273/A

9 781602 640139